THE CONNOLLY BOOK OF NUMBERS

VOLUME II

THE CONSULTANT'S MANUAL

THE CONNOLLY BOOK OF NUMBERS
VOLUME II
THE CONSULTANT'S MANUAL

EILEEN CONNOLLY

NEWCASTLE PUBLISHING CO., INC.
North Hollywood, California
1988

Edited by Douglas Menville
Charts by Peter Paul Connolly
Cover/Book Design by Riley K. Smith

FIRST EDITION
A NEWCASTLE BOOK
First printing, October 1988
10 9 8 7 6 5 4 3 2 1
Printed in the United States of America

ACKNOWLEDGMENTS

To my C.U.P. Graduate Students of California. With feet firmly in the Malkuth and clarity in the Kether, let beauty of being radiate from the center of who you are.

To my students and readers throughout the world, my sincere appreciation for your constant correspondence and kind thoughts. May this second volume of Gnothology be a welcome addition to your libraries.

I dedicate this book to my seventh grandchild:

ROSS PATRICK CONNOLLY

Born December 16, 1987 to Margaret and Jonathan Connolly.

OSP=1   OPV=6   OEK=7   OP=8   1ET=9

CONTENTS

LIST OF CHARTS

LIST OF MEDITATIONS

PREFACE

Here I am, as promised, at the harbor. I have another cargo for you to take aboard your ship of learning. Your sails of success are ready for another journey. It will be a long cruise, but you will have plenty to read and study along the way!

To enjoy this voyage you must have acquainted yourself with the fundamentals of the study of numbers. As we sail the high seas of your higher consciousness you will need to refer to the first book in this series, *The Connolly Book of Numbers, Vol. I: The Fundamentals*, which is still available from the publisher of the present volume. It will provide you with knowledge necessary to this study—your basic sea legs—as well as a vital continuity of comprehension.

The first volume covers the Major and Minor Mentors of the Basic Numbers ONE through NINE and the three Earthly Master Numbers (EMVs): *11, *22 and *33. It also covers procedures and Aspect Graphs for 44 of the 99 Gnothology Aspects; constructing your Personal Mantra and the Basic Gnothology Chart; composing the Karmic Block; analyzing the Basic Chart; and Meditations on numbers ONE through NINE are given as well.

Once you have mastered this maiden sea voyage, you will have returned with treasure that only you can fully appreciate and benefit from. Now you are ready for the next exploration—into the Cabalistic Regions, across the Ocean of Possibility, past the Rock of Consultancy and around the Isle of Study.

New and exciting horizons lie before you. With your two manuals, you are now ready to chart your course to new adventures as a Gnothology Consultant.

Again, my sincere appreciation to teachers, consultants and students all over the world who have found my previous works to be useful. I hope you will find this present volume equally helpful in your study of Gnothology.

Eileen Connolly
California
December 1987

INTRODUCTION

A *consultant* is a person who consults with another or others; an expert who is called upon for professional or technical advice or opinions. In Gnothology, the Consultant composes and delineates Natal Numerical Charts and interprets all their Aspects. He has a complete understanding of the flow of incoming and outgoing Cycles. He shares his conclusions with his clients, working always to assist and uplift them, offering his expertise and advice on esoteric matters dealing with karma and destiny.

This is a tremendous responsibility. The Gnothologist should recognize this fact and use the utmost sensitivity when giving any kind of counsel. With the basic fundamentals of Vol. I under your belt, I am sure that you are ready to assume this responsibility and continue your study to perfect your skills with numbers.

Have both volumes handy when charting your Aspects. Keep a notepad available to record any further bits of information you may obtain from in-depth charting. Analyze your Charts thoroughly before sitting down with your client to interpret them. Be prepared for questions from your client. If you are asked questions in a region you have not explored sufficiently, don't try to bluff your way through. Admit that you need to do more research and that you will find the answer for your client as soon as you can.

Everything is so exacting in this fascinating science of numbers. When relating your findings to your client, don't get so engrossed in the numerical Aspects that you forget to be human! Allow yourself to feel the highs and lows of the numerical vibrations, feel the vibratory frequencies you are conveying to your client. This can be achieved if you spend time in chart preparation and analysis prior to your client's visit.

You will want to expand your own Chart as you study the material in this second volume. I suggest you do this before you update any other Basic Charts you may be working with. You will be exploring the depths of Gnothology and learning how to connect particular Aspects to one another.

ASPECTS AND CHART PREPARATION

An ASPECT is a specific area of delineation on the Natal Gnothology Chart. There are 99 of these Aspects, 44 of which have been analyzed in the Basic Gnothology Chart, as demonstrated in Vol. I. The Major and Minor Mentors given there provide an introduction to the interpretation of these Aspects. This affords you a quick reference to any particular Aspect without having to go to the actual Chart.

Volume I shows how the Basic Chart should look when completed (see: Chapter 13, pp. 188–190). Volume II will expand into the remaining Aspects, which provide a deeper insight into Gnothology. These more complex delineation procedures will provide you with an extensive field of expertise. Together the two volumes of *The Connolly Book of Numbers* provide a full and comprehensive reference work for both the student and the practicing Consultant.

Each Aspect has a CODE which is written on the Graph when compiling the Gnothology Chart. These Codes provide quick references in identifying the many Aspects on the completed Chart. A complete list of these Aspects and their Codes will be given at the end of this Introduction.

The Gnothology Chart begins with the first of three CODE LEVELS: the O LEVEL. The O Level is the Level of the ORIGINAL FULL NAME AS GIVEN AT BIRTH and as listed on the birth certificate. Then the Chart extends to the next Level, the P LEVEL: THE NAME PRESENTLY BEING USED—the present vibrational status of the client to date. And finally, if relevant, you will work with the C

LEVEL: THE CHANGED NAME. This Level deals with periods during the client's time when other names or nicknames were used.

It is important to date the Chart when you complete the initial data. Number the pages of the Chart to keep the information in order. Each time you add any new Aspects to the Chart, date these additions.

The intensity of the Chart may be a result of the growth attained during a consultation; it may also be caused by the desire to penetrate every numerical possibility available. Your choice of Aspects should depend upon what information is required for the purpose of the consultation. I know some student Gnothologists who prefer to graph a complete Chart that includes every Aspect; others begin with the basic and advance the Chart according to the client's query and situation. Either way is all right, providing you are secure in your knowledge and experience. It's a matter of personal choice.

Updating Charts is essential, especially if you see a client on a regular basis. This will prepare you for any kind of question on present circumstances or future events.

Any notes or observations you make should not be written on the Chart. Rather, attach a separate sheet (also dated) and file it with the Chart. Neat and presentable Charts are easier to analyze and refer back to and look more impressive to a client. Remember not to use a ballpoint pen or felt-tip marker! Always use a pencil, for you'll be updating pertinent areas, and using a pencil and eraser saves you the trouble of redoing your Graphs.

Always take pride in your work; keep your Charts neat and legible. Practice with your own Chart. If you anticipate certain activities in the future, attach a note to your Chart to remind you. A fully completed Chart contains a lot of information. Cover your Charts with clear plastic holders and they will remain in excellent condition.

An excellent exercise is to practice reading and talking about your own Chart. Listen to yourself on a tape recorder. Explore all the areas of interpretation and then play back the tape; this will give you a good idea of how you explain things to your clients.

1. Are you believable?
2. Do you sound enthusiastic about the new incoming Cycles?
3. Do you fully explain the changes you expect to occur?

4. Do you get a good feeling of balance as each Aspect is discussed?

The advanced Gnothologist may want to consider making a written record of his analyses. This can be very helpful, especially with the O Levels. If a client wishes to have his information for reference, this written method is preferable for him, as he might have difficulty interpreting his own Chart.

Develop good habits as you go along and you will benefit greatly from them. Always use the Aspect Codes, as this will simplify your work and eliminate the likelihood of error in your interpretation. It will further assist you when analyzing from one Aspect to another. The Chart will then always be ready for consultation. The important Cycels to concentrate upon are:

1. Personal Life Cycles

2. Life Opportunities

3. Life Obstacles

4. Life Trinity Points

5. Transition Cycle Procedures

Now here is a complete list of all 99 Aspects, together with their Codes. You will note that the numbering is somewhat different from the list given in Volume I (see: Chapter 7, pp. 42–44); this is because of the necessity to add several more Aspects to each of the three sections: APPELLATIVE (Aspects taken from the vibratory frequencies of the *name*); PARTURITIVE (Aspects taken from the vibratory frequencies of the *birth*); and AMALGAMATIVE (Aspects taken from the *combined* vibratory frequencies of *name* and *birth*).

SECTION I: APPELLATIVE ASPECTS

CODE #	CODE	TITLE
1	OSP	Original Soul Print
2	OPV	Original Personality Vibration
3	OEK	Original Expressive Key
4	CSP	Change Soul Print

CODE #	CODE	TITLE
5	CPV	Change Personality Vibration
6	CEK	Change Expressive Key
7	PSP	Present Soul Print
8	PPV	Present Personality Vibration
9	PEK	Present Expressive Key
10	1ET	First Earth Tone
11	2ET	Second Earth Tone
12	CSB	Constant Soul Beat
13	IVP	Inner Vibratory Power
14	SS	Spiritual Seal
15	KOP1	Key to Original Plan #1
16	KOP2	Key to Original Plan #2
17	KOP3	Key to Original Plan #3
18	RE	Reflection
19	RK	Record of Karma
20	KL	Karma Lacking
21	KR	Karmic Response
22	PL	Past Lessons
23	PR	Personal Root Number
24	CB	Color Blocking
25	SA	Soul Affinity
26	KIB	Karmic Intention Block
27	SPB	Spectrum Block
28	SL1	Spectrum Level 1 (Age)
29	SL2	Spectrum Level 2 (First Name)
30	SL3	Spectrum Level 3 (Middle Name)
31	SL4	Spectrum Level 4 (Last Name)
32	MX	Spectrum Level 5 (Matrix)

SECTION II: PARTURITIVE ASPECTS

33	OP	Original Plan
34	CO	Commencement
35	VR	Vocational Roots
36	L.Opp 1	Life Opportunity #1
37	L.Opp 2	Life Opportunity #2

CODE #	CODE	TITLE
38	L.Opp 3	Life Opportunity #3
39	L.Opp 4	Life Opportunity #4
40	L.Obs 1	Life Obstacle #1
41	L.Obs 2	Life Obstacle #2
42	L.Obs 3	Life Obstacle #3 (Major Obstacle)
43	L.Obs 4	Life Obstacle #4
44	LT1	Life Trinity Point #1
45	LT2	Life Trinity Point #2
46	LT3	Life Trinity Point #3
47	AS	Astrological Sequence
48	CC	Christ Cycle
49	PLC	Personal Life Cycle
50	IMC	Individual Month Cycle
51	IDC	Individual Day Cycle
52	TU	Trinity Union
53	NTW	Natal Transition Wheel
54	MM	Monitor Month (Karmic Sun)
55	TG	Transition Grid
56	TMC	Transition Mystic Cycle
57	TB	Transition Birthday
58	ESD	Esoteric Seed Day
59	EKA	Exact Karmic Alignment
60	TJ	Transition Junctures
61	TI	Transition Impediments
62	BT	Balancing Tool
63	MBC	Mystic Birth Cycle
64	EB	Esoteric Birthday
65	TBC	Transition Bridge Cycle
66	NE	Nature of Essence
67	DVL	Daily Vibrational Level
68	NTT	Natal Transition Table
69	VX	Vertex
70	LG	Lunar Grid

SECTION III: AMALGAMATIVE ASPECTS

CODE #	CODE	TITLE
71	VM	Vocational Motivator
72	PT	Pranatic Total
73	SV	Strength Vibration
74	OCG	Original Commencement Goal
75	LR	Lineage Rooting
76	EST	Esoteric Trines
77	FG	Family Grid
78	RG	Relationship Grid
79	BG	Business Grid
80	TE	Triadic Expansion (Health Grid)
81	EBT	Esoteric Balancing Tool
82	AC	Activator
83	MO	Malefic Obligations
84	EE	Esoteric Expression
85	KE	Karmic Essence (Soul Structure)
86	EMV	Earthly Master Vibrations
87	HMV	Higher Master Vibrations
88	PST	Point of Stabilization
89	RN	Recognition Number
90	KRP	Karmic Replay
91	KP	Karmic Period
92	O.Lvl	Original Level
93	P.Lvl	Present Level
94	C.Lvl	Change Level
95	RR	Reverse Rooting
96	IR	Identical Rooting
97	TR	Two Rooting
98	PA	Present Age
99	MGV	Mutual Grid Vibrations

CHAPTER 1

THE INFLUENCE OF LETTERS

To begin our study of the *Consultant's Manual* we're going to examine each individual number more closely, in order to get more insight into its character and see how each number affects the other numbers on the Chart. By now you should have a pretty good idea of how to relate each number and all its possible influences. In this volume, we'll crack open the shell of each number like an egg and examine what's inside; you'll learn how to coordinate the essence of the number with your Aspect interpretations. This will give you additional insight, especially with the First Earth Tone (1ET).

BALANCING LETTERS

Almost as important as the numerical equivalents of the letters in a person's name are the letters themselves. As you study the individual characteristic of each letter, remember to use your sense of balance. In your previous studies you learned how essential it is to tune in to your client's spiritual and emotional vibrations. Recognizing the potential of each numerical vibration can greatly enhance your skill when consulting.

Consider the letters carefully. Observe how you make use of the vibratory level of each letter. Sometimes you'll find the vibrations good, sometimes bad, sometimes neutral. It all depends on what is happening in the person's life at the time.

For example, if you are inundated with "A's" in a Chart, and the person is offered a position of leadership, you should advise him to take it without hesitation. He will have all the inherent leadership qualities necessary for success in the position. On the other hand, if the vibrations are negative, your client might be on the defensive, feel insecure and behave in an aggressive and domineering manner. The third alternative would be the Stabilized Point, which is an exact balance between positive and negative influences.

Keep this in mind when analyzing a Chart. If there are unusual circumstances surrounding your client, then you may be able to anticipate which way he will react. On a normal day-to-day basis, like the weather in England, you can expect it to go one way or the other.

When a particular letter is repeated frequently in a name, you should pay attention to the implications of this. Look to the various areas of the Chart and keep the following in mind:

1. The influence of the letter will be more apparent if it is the FIRST letter of the FIRST name.

2. When it is the SECOND letter, you still have the energy pattern, but it can be hidden. It is good to activate the second letter whether it is a vowel or a consonant. If it is dormant, look for Aspects that are preventing an active balance. If it is overly active, look to the First Earth Tone (1ET) and you may find too much influence there.

3. Both FIRST and SECOND letter vibrations should be active. Each needs the support of the other to trigger a chain reaction throughout the full name.

4. As you observe the remaining letters in the name, note any repetitions of the FIRST letter. They will emphasize the vibratory influence, thereby strengthening the First Earth Tone. If the 1ET is inactive or submerged and the letter is repeated, these letters will not be functioning correctly. This can build up energy which can cause outbursts of temper and other negative reactions. Children especially respond quickly to inactive vibrations. If their 1ET is not being expressed or is repressed, the remaining vibrations can cause negative reactions such as oversensitivity.

INDIVIDUAL LETTER INFLUENCES

A vibrates to ONE

A repeated "A" signifies a go-getter in life. The more often it is found in the name, the more adventurous the person will be. Being the first letter in the English alphabet, the "A" carries a great sense of authority, but too many "A's" have a tendency to be overbearing. If distributed around the Chart more evenly, this influence is modified. The "A" person has great leadership qualities and is good at working alone.

B vibrates to TWO

"B" is an ideal partner, loving, giving and sensitive. They are tolerant people, yet they can be very unforgiving if they feel they have been wrongly treated. They have exceptional capacities for detail and memory and can recall situations long forgotten by most others. "B's" use their emotional level and often espouse deep philosophies. They are diligent workers and very loyal in relationships.

C vibrates to THREE

The abundant "C" vibrates with both physical and intellectual energy. Ideas bubble continually from them, sometimes without even thinking! The challenge of the THREE has its own resisting force, which is karmic. This force is a field of energy that must be used in the right way to overcome the Life Obstacles (L.Obs). When this is done, the results can be overwhelming! Talent and success go hand in hand with "C" people.

D vibrates to FOUR

Contained within the "D" is great potential, but the seeds of success are well insulated. The force of "D" can appear unbending to the world outside. The game of karma requires the "D's" to break their barriers and let the seasons of life nurture their seeds. The release key is the letter that follows. The second letter is often unnoticed, but its power can send the "D" exactly where it wants to go.

E vibrates to FIVE

The "E" is the catalyst. Each letter it touches becomes activated. It is the intellectual letter, representing all forms of communication. If repeated throughout the name it indicates much public exposure with words: acting, speaking, writing, etc. If it is the second letter in the first name, it should be carefully considered and not allowed to remain hidden.

F vibrates to SIX

Responsibility is found in the upright "F." As the first letter it denotes love of family and home. Coming as the second letter it indicates a need to protect one's affairs. A feeling of privacy prevails. First priority for the "F" is harmony in all things. However, this is not always good, for "F's" may tend to settle for less than they originally seeded for.

G vibrates to SEVEN

"G" gives the ability to contemplate. See how the letter curves and reaches for its own source. As a first letter it means a person who weighs everything carefully before arriving at a decision. As a second letter it acts as a brake! A safety barrier perhaps. Notice carefully where the SEVEN is placed: it should be a source of wisdom and not an obstacle.

H vibrates to EIGHT

Choice is always the dilemma of the "H". Obstacles seem to appear out of nowhere. There are always two ways to go. See the "H" as a stepladder. Earthly success continually presents choices. The "H" has a naturally pleasant personality unless he has stepped down! If "H" is not the first letter watch how it is used behind the scenes.

I vibrates to NINE

"I" is a universal symbol, concerned with the many. "I" people are both vulnerable and courageous. The "I" is unaffected by the other letters; its second letter can only be an alternative to the "I." It will rule the name, and if repeated you may see a very special person who is involved and concerned with everything except his own welfare. "I" people have a definite karmic destiny, an unbending purpose.

J vibrates to ONE

Increased vibratory energy comes from powerful "J" (10=1). You see magnetic force in its personality. The "J" has original ideas, something new to offer. "J" people can be bored if not in pursuit of their own concepts. As the first letter, "J" has a karmic purpose to express. If "J" appears as the second letter, there could be a personality like a volcano! Elsewhere in the name it will fire the 1ET to act.

K vibrates to TWO

A flair for living surrounds the "K." Dramatic situations appear to flow in and out of the life of "K"! Those born with "K" as a 1ET will see unusual activity. I would not suggest that "K" be adopted on a C Level. It is a very vibrant letter and its karmic suggestion is to succeed and answer a particular need left unfulfilled in a previous life. If "K" is the second letter, follow the direction of the 1ET to channel and form the "K."

L vibrates to THREE

"L" presents special qualities of character. Versatility is the gift of "L." Many talents will surface in this life, presenting many choices. Love is part of the "L's" daily diet. "L" people thrive on affection and return it in abundance. They are highly intuitive and dependable. As 1ET, "L" gives free-flowing thoughts. It is also good as the second letter and can be utilized anywhere in the name.

M vibrates to FOUR

"M" brings devotion to work, career and home and is the focal point in any family. Those with "M" will not be deterred from goals and will strive at any cost to achieve desired results. If "M" appears as the second letter, it will be somewhat modified, toned down. People with "M's" are lost if they don't feel a strong sense of purpose. They are loving and caring but have a tendency to be obstinate.

N vibrates to FIVE

"N" people are continually scanning. They receive magnificent ideas and before they can act upon them they receive more! As a first letter, "N" can bestow a quicksilver personality. "N" people may be scattered at times. They are always looking for the unusual and always ready to go. As a second letter or remaining letter, "N" can be inspiring and activate any sluggishness. Look for the power of the second letter to solidify an "N" 1ET. This gives a wonderful potential.

O vibrates to SIX

Within the esoteric circle of the SIX we can have all things. There is continual regrowth: Cycles within Cycles emanate from the SIX. The "O" means total balance in many things. Concentration is upon the home and family, but expansion beyond this priority can also be successful. As a second letter, allow its influence to penetrate the 1ET for stability and prosperity.

P vibrates to SEVEN

As the first letter, "P" has more going on inside than you can see! Once "P" people have found their purpose, they can burst into action and be certain of success. Until then they watch and learn with great clarity. They are the curious souls who want answers and silently set firm goals. As a second letter, "P" can be disconcerting, causing a constant inner struggle for release until perfectly assured.

Q vibrates to EIGHT

"Q" is another unusual vibration. Composed of the ONE with the SEVEN, the impact of the EIGHT adds its power wherever placed in the name. It is the extra energy required to achieve a definite purpose in this life, and should not be ignored or wasted. "Q" people generate a great amount of power and will not give up on their goals.

R vibrates to NINE

Past-life experience endows the first letter "R" with a level of determination that is exceptionally strong. While good if used correctly, it can be devastating if not! "R" people are single-minded, difficult to sway and have the ability to affect other people without them realizing it! The lesson for "R" is the law of perception. This strength lies only with the 1ET. As the second or remaining letter, it is like a booster shot when needed.

S vibrates to ONE

"S" people desire to be creative in an expansive way. It's difficult for them to think small! They can lead others and organize them to achieve their goals. They are creative leaders who like to do their own thing. If aroused they can be quite emotional; otherwise they have a good sense of control. As the second letter, "S" can be frustrating, for it is difficult to allow this energy to work behind the scenes.

T vibrates to TWO

"T" in the 1ET denotes high principles and devotion to a cause that involves the Higher Self. The "T" is like identical twins, each with their own emotional level and plagued by the agony of indecision. But if a "T" person is determined, there is no other letter that gives a greater bonding to another. "T" people will always give their best.

U vibrates to THREE

"U" is another special vibration with a karmic influence. The "U" 1ET has a quality of personality that is endearing. Many opportunities will come into being, but by the same token, many may be lost! The chalice quality of the "U" represents a vessel for receiving life's finest gifts. But if taken for granted the chalice will overflow. If it is the second letter, "U" adds zest to life.

V vibrates to FOUR

"V" has come to demonstrate knowledge learned in previous lifetimes. With precision and quality the components of TWO and TWO will provide the solid foundation on which "V" people can commence the hard work required to fulfill their destiny. As the second letter, "V" will fortify and strengthen the present purpose, for it's evident that great things have been accomplished in the last life.

W vibrates to FIVE

"W" is a vibration that carries unpredictable energies! The "W" wants change and will work toward that end. Speed is important, delays cannot be tolerated. Hopefully the second letter will modify the impulse of the "W." If "W" becomes the second letter, then undercurrents result in surprises and swiftness of action. "W" people are quick thinking and bright.

X vibrates to SIX

"X" is seldom used in the English language, but when used it generates an energy that benefits many. Ego as such cannot exist on this level. Consequently, the bearer of this name is concerned more with the many than himself. "X" bestows an outgoing, highly spiritual vibration that can influence generations to come. If the "X" person cannot or does not use the inherent esoteric energy, it will dissipate completely and the second letter will take precedent.

Y vibrates to SEVEN

The "Y" soul has returned to find its true purpose: to explore and discover the mystical connection between spheres of life. Writing will stimulate the higher self to release what "Y" people already know. Their personality is usually kind but withdrawn. Vocations are felt deeply by the "Y." As the second letter it provides a well of wisdom behind the 1ET.

Z vibrates to EIGHT

Potent ability and earth energy radiate from the "Z" 1ET. Power comes easily. The balance of the name indicates how it may be used. However, if the power is manifested but not used correctly it will disappear. Nevertheless, there is a wonderful opportunity to reach the pinnacle of success if past wisdom is used. As a second letter there will be a constant striving to achieve. The "Z" is directed from the 1ET.

CHAPTER 2

KARMIC INTENTION

In this chapter we will explore in greater depth and detail the relationship of letters and numbers to the various levels of the individual's karma. This Aspect is known as the KARMIC INTENTION BLOCK (KIB); it is listed as number 26 in the list of Aspects you will find in the Introduction to this volume.

Four levels of Karmic Intention are revealed through the given name at birth. By placing the letters of the name into each of these four categories you can determine where the person's strengths lie and their purpose. The four categories are:

1. Mental

2. Physical

3. Emotional

4. Intuitional

As you consider these categories, you should understand that they do not necessarily denote areas of expertise in this life; they show where the individual's energies *should be focused* to achieve the *original Karmic Intention*.

If you find that you are concentrating your energies in a category that is not related to your Karmic Intention, it's never too late to begin to use the energy from the category that can best help you achieve your original Karmic Intention. When you begin to apply energies from the correct category, you'll usually find that many obstacles and barriers will be overcome.

The soul has had the experience shown in the designated category. Upon discovering where the Karmic Intention lies, it requires thought and skill to decide how the source of karmic experience can be best utilized in this life. Therefore, as a Consultant you have a responsibility to study this area carefully before including it in a consultation.

LEVELS WITHIN LEVELS

Within each of the four main categories of Karmic Intention are three further levels. These levels explain *how* the energies from the four main categories can best be used. They are:

1. Beginner
2. Middle
3. Finisher

You can think of these three levels as a kind of relay race team:

1. Beginner = Starter (the man who begins the race)
2. Middle = Pickup (the man who grabs the baton and continues)
3. Finisher = Finisher (the man who finishes the race)

Beginner Level

This level is composed of those people who initiate new ideas and projects. They discover the seed and plant it. They are full of good ideas and intentions. Many leaders have this level.

Middle Level

This level propagates the seed; these people nourish and watch over the growth of new ideas and projects. They feel a need to contribute to the growth of something good and worthwhile. They are reliable and show good judgment; they will work hard and can use their own initiative once a project is put in their care.

Finisher Level

This level supervises and completes projects. These people are always ready to take over and bring something to a close. They won't waste their energy on a project, though, unless they are certain of achieving its completion. Their goals are very important and they will do almost anything to achieve them, even to the exclusion of other areas of their life.

THE KARMIC INTENTION BOX

As you work with this Aspect, each individual letter from the O LEVEL (original name as given at birth) name should be entered into the KARMIC INTENTION BOX (see page 15). This device will enable you to quickly and accurately organize all the information in one reference place.

Notice that each letter of the alphabet has its own place in the Box, so those letters in the person's name go in the same position. For example: In the MENTAL CATEGORY, BEGINNER LEVEL, the letter "A" appears. Therefore, any "A's" in the subject's name will go in that same position. As I did in Volume I, I'm once again using my son, Peter Paul Connolly, as the subject here. So, his name containing one "A," that letter will appear in the MENTAL/BEGINNER block of the Karmic Intention Box.

Likewise, any "E's" should go in the PHYSICAL/BEGINNER block; there are two in his name. There is one "T" in his name, so that goes into the EMOTIONAL/MIDDLE block. And the single "C" in his name appears in the INTUITIONAL/FINISHER block.

Now here are the areas designated for the various letters:

CATEGORY	LEVEL	LETTERS
Mental	Beginner	A
	Middle	H J N P
	Finisher	G L
Physical	Beginner	E
	Middle	W
	Finisher	D M

CATEGORY	LEVEL	LETTERS
Emotional	Beginner	I O R Z
	Middle	B S T X
	Finisher	None
Intuitional	Beginner	K
	Middle	F Q U Y
	Finisher	C V

Now you can study and understand how Peter's name has been entered into the Karmic Intention Box. The numerical equivalents of each letter are determined and added up to reach a total for each category. Peter's totals are:

1. Mental   =   8
2. Physical   =   2
3. Emotional   =   4
4. Intuitional   =   3

UNDERSTANDING THE KARMIC INTENTION BLOCK

In order to fully understand the meaning of the Karmic Intention Block (KIB), which is the *total* Aspect as recorded in the Karmic Intention Box, we need to use two Aspects as KEYS. The first is the ORIGINAL PLAN (OP). To examine any aspect of the Gnothology Chart you need to keep the OP firmly fixed in your mind, for everything you see on the Chart is aiming in that direction! You'll need the OP in order to penetrate the wisdom in each category and on each level of the KIB. As we determined in Volume I, Peter's OP = TWO (see: Chapter 11, p. 119).

The second Aspect to keep in mind as a KEY to interpretation is the VOCATIONAL ROOTS (VR). This Aspect will suggest ways of using the energy contained in the KIB. For Peter, we determined in Volume I that since his birthday is August 1, 1964, his VR is ONE = SCIENTIFIC (see: Chapter 11, p. 169). Now let's examine the categories and levels in more detail.

Peter Paul Connolly.   Karmic Intention Box = K18.   1987.

O P = R
V R = Scientific.

PETER PAUL CONNOLLY ✓✓✓✓ ✓✓✓✓✓

	Mental	Peter	Physical	Peter	Emotional	Peter	Intuitional	Peter
Beginner	A	A	E	E E	I O R Z R O O	K		*none
Middle	H J N P P N N	P P N N	N	*none	B S T X T	T	F R 4 Y U Y	
Finisher	G L	L L L	D M	*none	✓✓✓✓ C V	C	C	

Mental Beginner = A = 1
Mental Middle = P P N N = 4
Mental Finisher = L L L = 3

Physical Beginner = E E = 2
Physical Middle = none = 0
Physical Finisher = none = 0

Emotional Beginner = R O O = 3
Emotional Middle = T = 1
Emotional Finisher = no 3rd level exists.

Intuitional Beginner = none = 0
Intuitional Middle = 4 Y = 2
Intuitional Finisher = C = 1

Total: Mental = 8
Total: Physical = 2
Total: Emotional = 4
Total: Intuitional = 3

Note! As each level is analysed keep focus with the OP and VR.

Mental Category

These individuals have brought into this lifetime knowledge previously acquired but not used. The same circumstances can prevent them from initiating their knowledge again! A predominance of letters in this category (A/HJNP/GL) indicates that although this may indeed be possible, it is highly improbable, for their karmic path will be shared by those on other levels who can assist them in releasing their knowledge for the benefit of many.

Serious and beneficial seeds lie in their subconscious. They must be encouraged to release what they know and attract to themselves those people who can help to bring their seeds to fruition.

AREAS OF EXPERTISE

1. Leadership; control of large masses
2. New and enlightening techniques for human development
3. Educational and scientific progress
4. Writing works of international importance
5. Religious and/or political reform

NEEDS

1. To share their philosophy
2. To work out their ideas
3. To express views

Physical Category

These people are interested in progress and do not like procrastination. Results are vital to them; they will strive to improve humanity and want to paint the world in bright colors. They are the achievers and will study hard to achieve the results they need.

Their energy level is very high, being composed of thought and action. They are loyal, will work untiringly and can stick to the point without becoming distracted. They are ideally suited for executing detailed plans. Watch their body movements and you will see the electricity-like energy sizzle as they coordinate their ideas with their movements.

AREAS OF EXPERTISE

1. Good organizers
2. Excellent teachers; detailed and factual
3. Interested in creating and completing
4. Communication gifts; good ambassadors
5. No-nonsense personality; practical and thorough

NEEDS

1. To demonstrate their abilities
2. To fully complete their projects
3. To investigate, research and teach

Emotional Category

Decisions are based on emotional considerations; consequently, people in this category are exceptionally sensitive and concerned about others. They are the creative people: their tools are paint and canvas, camera and film, pen and paper. They are the poets, the artists, the architects, the many wonderful souls who contribute much beauty to the world.

These special people do not concern themselves much with logic or reason. Using their inborn sensitivity, they create the color, drama and excitement of life. Dreams and ideas flood their minds, but it is not always possible for them to bring to fruition what they feel inside. Nevertheless, they are a balancing force for the more prosaic, materialistic side of society, bringing with them talents acquired in previous lifetimes.

AREAS OF EXPERTISE

1. Understanding the needs of others
2. Art, music, writing, drama, filmmaking, dance

3. Adding sensitivity to harsh opinions and situations

4. Producing beauty, form and balance

5. Contributing insights when others are blinded by ambition

NEEDS

1. To share their unique ideas with the world

2. To have outlets for their creativity

3. To express their true purpose and talent

Intuitional Category

Sometimes these people appear to be far removed from the normal accepted patterns of behavior. This is because their thoughts are constantly drifting into other levels of comprehension and they become preoccupied with their own inner worlds. They can be truly inspiring, but they can also appear depressed. They can disconnect from reality and come up with alternatives for anything.

Once they become absorbed in any kind of study, they will pursue it until they obtain the results they need. They have a deep understanding and appreciation of religion and unusual philosophies. When they specialize in their own field, they make good teachers.

AREAS OF EXPERTISE

1. Teaching what they have learned

2. Giving love and understanding to those in need

3. Offering alternatives to difficult situations

NEEDS

1. To be open to communicate

2. To be aware of the student

3. To have schedules and sabbaticals

ANALYZING THE KARMIC INTENTION BLOCK

Analyzing this Aspect is not as easy and straightforward as for the previous Aspects we have studied. The reasons for this are:

1. Each individual letter has its own strength and interpretation.

2. There are vital differences in the personalities of each letter.

For example, let's take the three letters, "C," "L" and "U." Each of these letters vibrates to the number THREE—but they are not the same.

The Letter "C"

Hidden vibrations contribute to the beauty of "C." A strong psychic potential adds to the magic of the outgoing personality. "C" is filled with energy and intuition.

The Letter "L"

This letter is far more exacting! Intuition is focused on logic and reason, creating a clarity of expression based on a factual foundation. "L" is harnessed, yet not uncomfortable, and has a methodical outlook on things.

The Letter "U"

Here is an outgoing vibratory flow, as with "C" and "L." The difference here is the receptivity of the "U." However, as it receives it can overflow with enthusiasm and lose it all, so caution is necessary. "U" vibrates on a softer frequency than "C" and "L"; it is vulnerable and cooperative.

From these three examples you can see how important it is to analyze EACH LETTER SEPARATELY when working with the Karmic Intention Box. Each of the letters above vibrates to THREE, yet each does so in a very different manner from the others. You will find this to be true with all letters with the same numerical value.

Concentrated study on both NUMERICAL and ALPHABETI-CAL interpretation is vital if you are to master the Language of Numbers and become a skilled Consultant. Practice makes perfect! Your own Chart can become your training ground. You have the advantage of knowing yourself, so you are in the ideal position to tell whether your work results in an accurate analysis of who you are.

ADDITIONAL PERSONALITY TRAITS OF THE LETTERS

CATEGORY	LEVEL	LETTER	TRAITS
Mental	Beginner	A	Determination/Originality
	Middle	H	Decision/Indecision
		J	Sense of purpose/New ideas
		N	Imagination/Intellect
		P	Introversion/Curiosity
	Finisher	G	Reservation/Strength
	Finisher	L	Versatility/Methodicalness
Physical	Beginner	E	Inspiration/Science
	Middle	W	Impulsiveness/Generosity
	Finisher	D	Containment/Solidity
		M	Orderliness/Caution
Emotional	Beginner	I	Courage/Power
		O	Balance/Growth
		R	Perception/Leadership
		Z	Insight/Success
	Middle	B	Tolerance/Attention to detail
		S	Creativity/Emotion
		T	Spirituality/Energy
		X	Extroversion/Vulnerability
	Finisher	None	None

CATEGORY	LEVEL	LETTER	TRAITS
Intuitional	Beginner	K	Drama/Unusualness
	Middle	F	Responsibility/Privacy
		Q	Extremity/Potentiality
		U	Receptivity/Charm
		Y	Searching/Mysticism
	Finisher	C	Abundance/Production
		V	Knowledge/Precision

For further assistance in alphabetical interpretation, refer back to the last section of the previous chapter, "Individual Letter Influences."

CHAPTER 3

COMPOSING THE ADVANCED GNOTHOLOGY CHART

In Volume I we completed 44 Procedures for the various basic Aspects. In this chapter we will complete many of the remaining Aspects that were withheld until this volume because of the advanced nature of their charting and delineation. Procedures 45 through 54 will be shown in the same format you became accustomed to in the previous book. Other Aspects will be developed in more depth, as was the Karmic Intention Block (KIB) in the last chapter.

The Transition Section includes various Aspects that are needed to complete the Transition Period. They will be included in Chapters 4 through 7.

PROCEDURES

The Procedure for each Aspect is numbered and contains the following information:

1. Procedure Number
2. Aspect Title
3. Aspect Code (Chart Code)
4. Divinatory Section
5. Source
6. Aspect Information

7. Calculation

8. Description

9. Aspect Graph

Please note that the numbering of the Aspects in the PROCEDURE INDEX that follows is *not* the same as in the chart in the Introduction, nor do the Aspects follow in the same order.

PROCEDURE INDEX

	CODE	TITLE	SOURCE	SECTION
45.	PR	Personal Root Number	Name	Appellative
46.	CB	Color Blocking	Name	Appellative
47.	TU	Trinity Union	Birth	Parturitive
48.	SA	Soul Affinity	Name	Appellative
49.	LR	Lineage Rooting	Combined	Amalgamative
50.	EST	Esoteric Trines	Combined	Amalgamative
51.	TE	Triadic Expansion (Health Grid)	Combined	Amalgamative
52.	EBT	Esoteric Balancing Tool	Combined	Amalgamative
53.	EE	Esoteric Expression	Combined	Amalgamative
54.	KE	Karmic Essence (Soul Structure)	Combined	Amalgamative

PROCEDURE 45

ASPECT TITLE: PERSONAL ROOT NUMBER

ASPECT CODE: PR

SECTION: Appellative

SOURCE: Name

ASPECT INFORMATION:

The PR is derived through an inverted triadic Cabalistic formula. It is the key to the Astral Self and can bring 100 percent efficiency when you are balanced. You should delineate the PR immediately and approach *every* Level through its nature and essence. It is *first* linked with the OP and identifies the form of energy used to reach this Aspect. When the PLC is identical to the PR, the combined vibrations project the true nature clearly. The PR number can be considered a lucky one if the client is balanced properly. Sensitivity and direction join together to produce this vital Aspect.

CALCULATION:

Use only the FIRST NAME as given at birth and follow the eleven steps as given in the Aspect Graph below. (Note: With Peter Paul Connolly, the PR is delineated using only PETER.)

DESCRIPTION:

Difficulty in communication can be helped considerably by using the PR energy. People usually respond quickly when this approach is used; it's good for in-depth counselling.

ASPECT GRAPH:*

Personal Root Number = PR = 5

		P	E	T	E	R
1.	Write first name	P	E	T	E	R
2.	Numerical value for each letter	7	5	2	5	9
3.	Add 7+5, 5+2, 2+5, 5+9		12/3	7	7	14/5
4.	Place totals of additions with Rooting.		12/3	7	7	14/5
5.	Add 3+7, 7+7, 7+5					
6.	Place totals of additions with Rooting.			6	8	
7.	Add 1+5, 5+3			14		
8.	Place totals of additions with Rooting.			5	= PR.	
9.	Add 6+8					
10.	Place total of addition with Rooting.					
11.	Add 1+4 equals 5 PR.					

*Before you attempt this Procedure, you may wish to review Vol. I, Chapter 4, "Rooting the Numbers."

PROCEDURE 46

ASPECT TITLE: COLOR BLOCKING

ASPECT CODE: CB

SECTION: Appellative

SOURCE: Name

ASPECT INFORMATION:

Color Blocking is for the NAME ONLY, on all Levels—O, C and P. CB shows us the *intensity* of the name. Under each letter goes the appropriate color as chosen from the Balance Scale. (Review Vol. I, Chapter 6, "Your Personal Mantra," p. 33.) To see the power of the name, you stack the colors like children's blocks, starting with the most influential color (the one that appears most often) and building upward accordingly. Do this first for the O Level; then do the other Levels for comparison. You will immediately see the changes in strength as you Color Block each level.

CALCULATION:

Color the block beneath each letter of the FULL NAME according to the color values of the Balance Scale. Color Block the total of the OSP, which is known as the SOUL COLOR. Wearing the OSP color helps to express inner qualities, but avoid it if you're feeling vulnerable. Wear the OEK color to bring out how you feel and what you want. When the OEK and OSP colors are identical, the level of sensitivity is reduced. (Note: Use colored pencils for this operation, if at all possible.)

DESCRIPTION:

Wearing the OSP and OEK colors gives additional energy needed for important occasions such as dates, interviews, etc. Choosing the right Aspect and wearing its color can give you added confidence.

EXAMPLE: (Arranged vertically for convenience)

P	=	7	=	Violet	OSP	=	8	=	Rose Pink
E	=	5	=	Blue	OEK	=	8	=	Rose Pink
T	=	2	=	Orange					
E	=	5	=	Blue					
R	=	9	=	Gold					

(Continue with PAUL and CONNOLLY.)

PROCEDURE 47

ASPECT TITLE: TRINITY UNION

ASPECT CODE: TU

SECTION: Parturitive

SOURCE: Birth

ASPECT INFORMATION:

This Aspect is delineated for compatibility between two people. It gives three pieces of information regarding their relationship: physical, mental and vocational. The relationship concerned need not be man and wife—it can be any two people who are in close contact with each other: friends, family members, co-workers, etc. The resulting vibration for each person shows *how* they react to each other in each of the three categories. You must remember that the relationship may be positive, negative or stabilized.

CALCULATION:

1. Subtract one partner's BIRTH MONTH from the other's BIRTH MONTH. This gives you the number of the PHYSICAL relationship.
2. Subtract one partner's BIRTH DATE from the other's BIRTH DATE. This gives you the number of the MENTAL relationship.
3. Subtract one partner's OP number from the other's OP. This gives you the number of the VOCATIONAL relationship.

DESCRIPTION:

If the PHYSICAL number is ZERO, the two people have been together before, in a past life or lives. If the MENTAL number is ZERO, they should have a lot in common in this life. If the VOCATIONAL number is ZERO, they have a karmic link.

ASPECT GRAPH:

Trinity Union = TU.				
Peter Birth Month	=	8	Eileen =	5
Peter Birth Date	=	1	Eileen =	3
Peter Original Plan	=	2	Eileen =	22*
Physical relationship	=	8 − 5 = 3	=	3
Mental relationship	=	3* − 1 = 2	=	2
Vocational relationship	=	22* − 2 = 20/2	=	2

PROCEDURE 48

ASPECT TITLE: SOUL AFFINITY

ASPECT CODE: SA

SECTION: Appellative

SOURCE: Name

ASPECT INFORMATION:
> This is another Procedure to use when considering the compatibility between two people. It is a simple calculation, yet it reveals a depth of understanding which opens up a completely new area of consulting. It defines a point of communication that will always remain open between the two individuals. Relationships of any kind can prosper if this level of communication is used. Making a simple triad and using its three points to place the numbers will keep the SA Procedure clear on your Chart.

CALCULATION:
> Add together the OSP numbers of the two people concerned. Reduce the total to a single digit (unless it is an EMV) and place it at the apex of the triad on the Chart.

DESCRIPTION:
> When there is a need for true communication, it should be channelled through the Soul Affinity, especially when the people concerned are experiencing difficulty in communicating with each other.

ASPECT GRAPH:

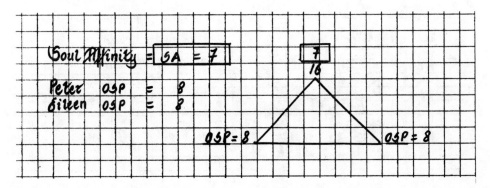

PROCEDURE 49

ASPECT TITLE: LINEAGE ROOTING

ASPECT CODE: LR

SECTION: Amalgamative

SOURCE: Combined

ASPECT INFORMATION:

This Aspect is an excellent guideline for the Consultant. It shows clearly other Aspects that contain great strength, and that should not be treated lightly or overlooked. The purpose of the LR is to emphasize Aspects in this life that will be stressed and tested more than the regular vibrations. When analyzing a Chart you will see *why* the LR's are placed where they are. They provide the acceleration needed to accomplish the goals associated with the original Karmic Intention. The placement of LRs indicates where strength should be applied and shows a deep desire for achievement in that area of the Chart. More than one LR intensifies the purpose.

CALCULATION:

LR numbers are derived when calculating any of the other Aspects. The two examples given below are from Peter's Original Purpose (OP) and Strength Vibration (SV).

DESCRIPTION:

A source of strength and purpose is found whenever a Lineage Rooting number appears in the calculation of Aspects.

ASPECT GRAPH:

Lineage Rooting = LR.

Two examples:

August	=	8
Day	=	1
Year	= 1 9 5 4	

1 9 7 3 = LR = 20 = OP 2.

OP R = 8
O.P. = 2
10 = LR = 1 SV.

Lineage Rootings = 10 / 1   20 / 2   30 / 3   40 / 4   50 / 5   60 / 6   70 / 7   80 / 8   90 / 9

PROCEDURE 50

ASPECT TITLE: ESOTERIC TRINES

ASPECT CODE: EST

SECTION: Amalgamative

SOURCE: Combined

ASPECT INFORMATION:

There are four types of Esoteric Trines:

1. Physical
2. Strength
3. Social (Extrovert)
4. Concealed (Introvert)

The following numbers indicate the type of Esoteric Trine:

1. Physical   =   1   6   *11
2. Strength   =   2   7   12/3
3. Social   =   3   8   9
4. Concealed   =   4   10/1   5

Esoteric Trine numbers can *only* be extracted from the following Aspects:

1. OSP	7. SV	13. IVP
2. OPV	8. AC	14. OP
3. OEK	9. PT	15. AS
4. 1ET	10. KOP1	16. OCG
5. 2ET	11. KOP2	17. CO
6. CSB	12. KOP3	18. VM
		19. VR

Each Esoteric Trine gives added emphasis to a particular area of a person's life. The ancients considered the Trine to be a mark of success if used in accordance with the area of emphasis. It is the result of a complex Cabalistic formula and today can be considered "lucky" if used in accordance with the correct area of emphasis of each Trine. However, this luck will only become evident if the person works on that particular Aspect when it has been revealed to him.

The Physical Trine

The PHYSICAL TRINE is composed of a total of SIX numbers, two each of: 1 6 *11. Therefore, in order to justify a Physical Trine, you must have:

1. TWO ONES
   plus
2. TWO SIXES
   plus
3. TWO *ELEVENS

The Physical Trine emphasizes RESPONSIBILITY.

ONES	=	Stamina, health, healing, personal charisma
SIXES	=	Exceptional mental qualities, original philosophies, the urge to travel
*ELEVENS	=	Highly developed intuition, compassion toward all; should derive much pleasure from this life

The Strength Trine

The STRENGTH TRINE is composed of a total of SIX numbers, two each of: 2 7 12/3 (Note: The THREE *must be* Rooted 12/3). To justify a Strength Trine, you must have:

1. TWO TWOS
   plus
2. TWO SEVENS
   plus
3. TWO THREES Rooted with ONE and TWO

The Strength Trine reveals KARMIC GIFTS EARNED.

TWOS	=	Exceptional power to attract what is needed; magnetism, ability to succeed
SEVENS	=	Gift of healing self and others Powerful gift of healing nature
THREES (1+2)	=	Ability to concentrate and manifest prosperity in all material things

The Social Trine

The SOCIAL TRINE is composed of a total of SIX numbers, two each of: 3 8 9. To justify a Social Trine, you must have:

1. TWO THREES
   plus
2. TWO EIGHTS
   plus
3. TWO NINES

The Social Trine emphasizes RELATIONSHIPS.

THREES	=	Drawn into relationships, karmic experiences; many situations, both good and bad
EIGHTS	=	Unusual contacts made through short journeys; writing, studying, a message to reveal
NINES	=	Compassion, helping others in need, ability to achieve great status in this lifetime

The Concealed Trine

The CONCEALED TRINE is composed of a total of SIX numbers, two each of: 4 10/1 (Note: The ONE *must be* Rooted 10/1). To justify a Concealed Trine, you must have:

1. TWO FOURS
   plus

2. TWO ONES Rooted with ONE and ZERO
   plus
3. TWO FIVES

The Concealed Trine reveals what is HIDDEN. It must be carefully sought after and can be most beneficial, but can also create disappointment if not used correctly.

FOURS = Hidden opportunities always available in areas of finance, such as banking and real estate

ONES (1+0) = Partners, legacies, wills, finances; requires an independent approach and attitude

FIVES = Control, working within boundaries; if overly activated, can cause restriction and regret

DESCRIPTION:

The four Esoteric Trines have their own individual purposes and are comprised of certain numbers found in Aspects 1 through 19. Beyond the list of interpretations given above for these numbers, there are some people who have additional Aspects that contribute toward the making of additional Trines. This exclusive group is well equipped to become very successful and to contribute to the welfare and happiness of others. They feel that they have a firm grip on life. These souls are very special and will give light in whatever environment they exist. Many young people are now coming in with these exceptional esoteric qualities: they will be the future teachers, leaders and humanitarians. Having experienced many lifetimes of struggle and toil, they now come to benefit themselves and others. They have important things to say and do and their secrets lie within the Esoteric Trines.

PROCEDURE 51

ASPECT TITLE: TRIADIC EXPANSION (HEALTH GRID)

ASPECT CODE: TE

SECTION: Amalgamative

SOURCE: Combined

ASPECT INFORMATION:

The purpose of the Triadic Expansion is to extract all the numbers from the Analysis Block* and arrange them into THREE sections:

1. 1   2   3
2. 4   5   6
3. 7   8   9

Each triad of numbers can then be considered for certain characteristics, both *positive* and *negative*. These personality traits act like a magnet and will become evident under certain circumstances.

1   2   3

POSITIVE: Maintains own individuality in any undertaking.

NEGATIVE: Becomes aggressive and selfish.

4   5   6

POSITIVE: Will give to many and work well toward goals.

NEGATIVE: Disorganized, lazy, avoids responsibilities.

7   8   9

POSITIVE: High intellect, likes new things, is unafraid.

NEGATIVE: Introverted, scatters energies, uncoordinated.

*See: Vol. I, Chapter 13, p. 197.

DESCRIPTION:

The results of your analysis will often be the Point of Stabilization. The extremes are obvious, and the Triadic Expansion will allow you to categorize your findings immediately. From the TE you can then explore the various Aspects, see how they are functioning and determine what is causing any imbalance. Ask questions and see how the vulnerable Aspects are reacting to everyday pressures. The TE clearly shows where the first signs of pressure are appearing by the accumulation of numerical energies.

Health Grid

INFORMATION:

The HEALTH GRID is compiled *after* you have determined the Triadic Expansion. It is best to consider this procedure as part of the TE—an expansion that shows how the negative characteristics affect the physical body. When there is an imbalance within the esoteric structure of the body, the physical body quickly reacts! Tension and pressure create a vibratory rate that is not conducive to well-being. These vibrations find their outlet in the physical parts of the body that relate to each part of the Triadic Expansion. These relationships are:

1. HEAD   = 3 6 9
2. HEART   = 2 5 8
3. STOMACH = 1 4 7

WHERE YOUR PREDOMINANCE OF NUMBERS APPEARS WILL DETERMINE THE PHYSICAL REACTION WHEN UNDER STRESS OR TENSION.

DESCRIPTION:

I'm sure you've heard people say things like, "I'm under the weather" or "out of sorts," etc. Preliminary physical deterioration begins this way. If you have charted a person who expresses these feelings often, you will probably recognize why he talks this way. The source of discomfort usually begins in one or more of the three areas listed above. To remove the initial discomfort, he must take some action regarding the reason for it. This will alleviate the physical stress and allow him to solve the problem which is creating the illness. Negativity will only increase the discomfort in physical areas; a positive attitude will add strength and promote healing in these areas. Good thoughts and objective planning will release the pressure. The physical areas will receive healing vibrations when the Aspects in the Triadic Expansion have been properly balanced.

PROCEDURE 52

ASPECT TITLE: ESOTERIC BALANCING TOOL

ASPECT CODE: EBT

SECTION: Amalgamative

SOURCE: Combined

ASPECT INFORMATION:

The EBT is invaluable when making an analysis of a Chart. It can help you understand how the varying numerical Aspects can work together to flow and continue from one another. With this Tool you can create and maintain a balance within the Chart whenever the Cycles appear to conflict. This balance can be retained when Cycles are in actual transition from one to another by the use of the EBT. This Tool may also be used when making an analysis concerning the compatibility of two people. It can help you explain how two opposite Cycles or Aspects can still work together smoothly and easily. When the EBT is used for comparison and compatibility it is extremely helpful.* As you study the Charts, a clean sheet of paper should be used for delineating the Esoteric Balancing Tool.

CALCULATION:

A good example of using the EBT might be as follows: A person is undergoing some difficulty in changing his Personal Life Cycle (PLC). He has enjoyed the harmony and balance of his PLC of SIX and is not looking forward to a year with the depths of the SEVEN. How is this person going to cope with this situation?

$$\begin{array}{r} \text{PLC of } 6 \\ + \\ \underline{\text{PLC of } 7} \\ 13 \ (1 + 3 = 4) \end{array}$$

*The EBT will be discussed further in Chapter 10.

This gives him a FOUR ESOTERIC BALANCING TOOL.

The changeover of Cycles will be satisfactory if the person uses the strength of the FOUR during the process. If there are Rootings of the EBT, as here with 1 + 3, these will indicate *how* the EBT should be used. By expressing his own individuality and being prepared to build new foundations from this Rooting, he will soon begin to feel comfortable with the incoming PLC of SEVEN.

Other Examples of the EBT

WITH ONE CHART

TRANSITION		EBT	CHARACTERISTIC
From L.Obs #2 to L.Obs #1	=	3	= Versatility
From OSP 6 to PSP 5	=	*11	= Intuition
From L.Opp #9 to L.Opp #5	=	14 (Rooting)	= 5 (See below)

When you see a Rooting (1+4), this indicates the way in which the EBT should be used. In the last example above, the Rooting shows that the emphasis is upon individuality (ONE) monitoring itself and creating new foundations with the FOUR. From this, the person will be able to express the freedom-loving nature of the FIVE.

BETWEEN TWO PEOPLE

The same procedure is used. If two people are not getting along well, the EBT can be applied in various Aspect areas. For example:

1. ADD the two OPVs together. This will indicate how the couple can adjust to an outgoing personality.
2. ADD the two OEKs together. This will show how they can improve their relationship.

To Analyze a Change of Levels

When a person changes his name, and the value of the Original Level is lessened, it can be supplemented to a degree by using the EBT. This makes extra work on the Chart, but if the person insists on using a new name, then it is a worthwhile procedure for you to undertake.

1. ADD the OSP and CSP
2. ADD the OPV and CPV
3. ADD the OEK and CEK

From these additions you will derive three EBTs, each of which will show you where effort is needed to support this Level Change. As long as the EBTs are consciously used, this should lessen the impact of the name change.

DESCRIPTION:

The EBT bridges many gaps. It can be used in numerous ways to improve your understanding and skill and for the benefit of your clients. I recommend that you use it whenever and wherever needed. The EBT can make an invaluable contribution to your analyses.

PROCEDURE 53

ASPECT TITLE: ESOTERIC EXPRESSION

ASPECT CODE: EE

SECTION: Amalgamative

SOURCE: Combined

ASPECT INFORMATION:

This Procedure is intricate and requires both concentration and skill. As a Consultant you should familiarize yourself with it for use whenever in-depth counselling is called for or where there is an obvious need to boost the Chart with additional energy.

CALCULATION:

1. First, examine the Analysis Block to discover which vibratory levels are limited or missing entirely. If these limited or missing numbers are apparent in the lifepath of the client, you can use the EE Procedure to supplement his Chart.

2. Next, look to see where there is an abundance of any one number. *Only solidified vibrations* can be used here; not Rooted numbers. For example:

YES	NO
$5 + 4 = 9$	$7 + 6 = 13 = 4$

3. Combine the abundant numbers until you can total the missing number. For example, say your client is missing SEVENS. You find that he has five FOURS and four THREES. If you add one of the FOURS to one of the THREES, you get SEVEN —his missing number.

$$4 + 3 = 7$$

4. Your next step is to *look closely* at the Aspects from which you derived the abundant numbers of FOUR and THREE. Let's assume you extracted them from the following Aspects:

CSB	=	4	OPV	=	3

By combining these numbers and creating an EE for your client, you will cause an increase of energy in those two Aspect areas which he can begin to use immediately. The use of an EE does *not* draw any energy from the Original Level.

5. To explain the use of the additional SEVEN energy to your client, you would show him how it can be utilized in his present lifestyle. In this instance you can see that by adding depth to his thoughts and actions and by being a little more conservative and self-sufficient, he will be able to better understand his CSB of FOUR. The personality he projects will benefit from this understanding, and others may begin to take him more seriously.

6. The EE becomes 100 percent effective after a period of NINE WEEKS AND SEVEN MINUTES from the acknowledgement of its existence.

7. Once the client starts to use your advice, the EE is recorded in the Analysis Block in the SEVEN section. Use your pencil to draw a broken line around the number's box in the graph to indicate that you are waiting for it to become a permanent part of the Chart. When the time period is up and the EE has been used successfully, record it permanently by adding an asterisk (*) to it.

8. The source of the energy determines *where* the EE will be used. In this case, the CSB is more apparent, so the personality will have the added depth of the SEVEN.

9. If an EE *cannot* be delineated, then the person concerned can achieve his goals and solve his problems using his present numerical structure.

DESCRIPTION:

I suggest that you study this advanced Aspect using your own Chart first. If you have missing numbers, then you can go through the process personally. With this experience you'll have first-hand knowledge of how effective the EE can be, how the new energy provides a means for improving your lifestyle.

PROCEDURE 54

ASPECT TITLE: KARMIC ESSENCE (SOUL STRUCTURE)

ASPECT CODE: KE

SECTION: Amalgamative

SOURCE: Combined

ASPECT INFORMATION:
There is a vital connection between the OSP and the OP. Together they present the skeletal frame of the soul as it is melded with the OP. This becomes the actual essence which contains the true person. The KE is a vulnerable and revealing Aspect. If you attempt to threaten this structure, there will be a strong rejection which could create terrible friction in the Chart. IF the OSP and OP have the same numbers, you are confronted with extraordinary power. This power can generate an absolutely clear path of destiny. On the other hand, if not used with moderation, it can create an aggressive force which can detract from and delay all plans for achievement.

CALCULATION:
ADD the ORIGINAL SOUL PRINT number to the ORIGINAL PLAN number. The total gives you the number of the KARMIC ESSENCE. When the KE is identical to other Aspects, it will also be recognized in the outward expression of those Aspects.

DESCRIPTION:
The KE allows access to the inner person. It is a sensitive Aspect that is used frequently between loved ones and can be touched upon unknowingly during arguments or disagreements.

ASPECT GRAPH:

Karmic Essence = KE   Soul Structure

OSP = 8
OP = 2

Note! Peter has several "ones" which his KE amplifies.

10 = 1 KE

CHAPTER 4

THE TRANSITION PERIOD

The TRANSITION PERIOD is a fascinating and rewarding study. During the vital Transition Months you are able to see your Path of Destiny in perspective. Much is happening during this limited period of time: relationships become bonded or are dissolved due to the intensity of the many-faceted Cycles.

At this time you come face to face with life situations. Old ideas become outdated and new goals become feasible. There is often an internal struggle to decide whether to cling to the outmoded past or to associate yourself with the new incoming possibilities. The choices confront you and your reluctance shows itself plainly.

Transition is a time of realization. Inner yearnings surface and the Higher Self summons up all the energy available in order to alert you to your individual path of true destiny. You will find that hearts become more open, more generous, but tongues become more acid; a sense of reality descends upon us all during this crucial Transition Period.

Following the natural rhythm of the vibrational frequencies can bring you vivid pictures of your present status, visions which can provide inspiration for you to draw upon. The Period of Transition is a time to stop, think and act upon the living truth that is within you.

Somehow, once you accept the light of reality, it's not too difficult to adjust to it. *Everyone* undergoes the dominant aspects of Transition: we can see the Cycles at work everywhere, and not just with individuals. Organizations, governments, even nations are all affected by the surge of changing Cycles. A child, an adult, a business, governmental policies, all become part of the Transition, with Cycles colliding, merging, now speeding things up, now slowing them down, each according to the level.

Learning to know and understand the Cycles of Transition is not difficult. As a Consultant, you must become knowledgable in this area, as the information will assist you enormously in providing the answers your clients are seeking.

Consider the Months of Transition and how they affect present plans and activities. January 8 of each year is the foundation stone. It is from this point that the client can see his future plans. If during Transition he has understood the changing process, he will then be ready to proceed with his plans during the coming year. Any confusion in his mind is nothing more than the need to make decisions!

Transition is an excellent time of the year. It signals the start of new things and contains the promise of all that you desire. When the blindfold of insecurity is removed, the vision of your success shines bright and clear.

INDEX OF TRANSITION ASPECTS

Please note that the numbering of the Aspects for this Chapter is *not* the same as in the chart in the Introduction. All of these Aspects, plus the ones studied in the following chapters, will be used in deciphering the events of the Transition Period. With *all* of the following Aspects, the SOURCE is BIRTH and the SECTION is PARTURITIVE.

	CODE	TITLE
1.	MM	Monitor Month (Karmic Sun)
2.	TB	Transition Birthday
3.	NE	Nature of Essence
4.	TG	Transition Grid
5.	TMC	Transition Mystic Cycle
6.	MBC	Mystic Birth Cycle
7.	ESD	Esoteric Seed Day

8. DVL   Daily Vibrational Level
9. EKA   Exact Karmic Alignment
10. VX   Vertex

PERSONAL LIFE CYCLES AND INDIVIDUAL MONTH CYCLES

Before you go farther, you may want to refer back to Vol. I, Chapter 8, "The Influence of Cycles" (pp. 45–50). Keep these three facts firmly in mind as you study Cycles:

1. TRANSITION BEGINS EACH YEAR ON OCTOBER 1.

2. TRANSITION ENDS EACH YEAR AT MIDNIGHT, JANUARY 7.

3. THE PERSONAL LIFE CYCLE IS ACTIVATED AT 100% EFFICIENCY EACH YEAR FROM JANUARY 8 THROUGH SEPTEMBER 30.

In Vol. I I explained that SEPTEMBER is the month when both the PLC and the IMC are identical. The impact of these two Cycles is felt by everyone, in order to motivate each individual to achieve the purpose of the Personal Life Cycle.

Those with MASTER PLCs of *11, *22 and *33 will experience the reduced vibrations of 2, 4 and 6 respectively as the Individual Month Cycles during September each year.

Monitor Month

The MONITOR MONTH (MM) (October) is the month that previews the coming year: you begin the adapt to the incoming PLC. Each October you experience an IMC that is identical to the *next* PLC. For example:

A PLC of 1 would experience an IMC of 2 in OCTOBER.

A PLC of 2 would experience an IMC of 3 in OCTOBER.

A PLC of 3 would experience an IMC of 4 in OCTOBER.

A PLC of 4 would experience an IMC of 5 in OCTOBER.

A PLC of 5 would experience an IMC of 6 in OCTOBER.

A PLC of 6 would experience an IMC of 7 in OCTOBER.

A PLC of 7 would experience an IMC of 8 in OCTOBER.

A PLC of 8 would experience an IMC of 9 in OCTOBER.

A PLC of 9 would experience an IMC of 1 in OCTOBER.

A PLC of *11 would experience an IMC of 3 in OCTOBER.

A PLC of *22 would experience an IMC of 5 in OCTOBER.

A PLC of *33 would experience an IMC of 7 in OCTOBER.

Each PLC is given this Monitor Month to preview and gain insight into the year ahead and how the new PLC energies can be applied in our lives.

Twice each year the IMC is identical to the INCOMING CYCLE of the FOLLOWING YEAR. This occurs

1. In JANUARY, at the beginning of each year; and again

2. In OCTOBER of each year.

As soon as we enter a new year, therefore, we are confronted with an IMC which is identical to next year's PLC.

The Karmic Sun

In JANUARY of each year, THE KARMIC SUN comes into exact focus. This vibratory effect provides a unique sensitivity which alerts the higher consciousness and causes it to look within. Karmic behavior patterns become more clearly defined and the conscious mind is better able to receive knowledge from the higher source, thereby giving direction and guidance for the new PLC activating in January.

Under the influence of the Karmic Sun's heightened level of sensitivity, the *real you* can emerge. The challenge is not to lose sight of who you really are or where your capabilities lie. Open up and be receptive to the bold new patterns presented by your Higher Self during January.

The Karmic Sun is the term used to explain the high ratio of vibratory influences that occur each year due to the fixed Aspects concentrating specifically on your past-life patterns. The awareness of this force should become part of your recognition of the incoming PLC. This accounts for the urge to make new resolutions during this period. It is a time of new beginnings.

The Karmic Sun has its most exact effect on the first day of the MYSTIC BIRTH CYCLE (MBC), which begins on JANAURY 1 and sustains its influence for the FIRST SEVEN DAYS OF JANUARY. This is an ideal period to reflect on the past. Your Higher Self is conditioned to search and probe inward for insights that will prove helpful to you. It is also an excellent time for past-life therapy and regression.

Duplication of Cycles

During the month of SEPTEMBER the PLC and IMC are *duplicated*, creating a force of energy which directs you toward the purpose contained within *both* PLCs—the present one and the one incoming. This September energy lasts throughout the month, subsiding at MIDNIGHT, SEPTEMBER 30. The current PLC vibrations then begin to decrease as the incoming PLC vibrations begin to increase and develop daily.

Now let's look at each year's sequence of IMCs and PLCs and how they relate to each other. I have highlighted the interaction of both Cycles at the three important times of the year: January (Karmic Sun), September (duplication of Cycles) and October (Monitor Month). Note that wherever the IMC equates to an Earthly Master Vibration (EMV) that number is *not reduced*. These indicate special months during which greater insight regarding future action can be received.

Interaction of PLCs and IMCs

PLC of 1				PLC of 2		
Jan =	1 + PLC 1 =	2 IMC**	Jan =	1 + PLC 2 =	3 IMC**
Feb =	2 + PLC 1 =	3 IMC	Feb =	2 + PLC 2 =	4 IMC
Mar =	3 + PLC 1 =	4 IMC	Mar =	3 + PLC 2 =	5 IMC

Apr =	4 + PLC 1 =	5 IMC	Apr =	4 + PLC 2 =	6 IMC
May =	5 + PLC 1 =	6 IMC	May =	5 + PLC 2 =	7 IMC
Jun =	6 + PLC 1 =	7 IMC	Jun =	6 + PLC 2 =	8 IMC
Jul =	7 + PLC 1 =	8 IMC	Jul =	7 + PLC 2 =	9 IMC
Aug =	8 + PLC 1 =	9 IMC	Aug =	8 + PLC 2 =	1 IMC
Sep =	9 + PLC 1 =	1 IMC**	Sep =	9 + PLC 2 =	*11 IMC**
Oct =	1 + PLC 1 =	2 IMC**	Oct =	1 + PLC 2 =	3 IMC**
Nov =	*11 + PLC 1 =	3 IMC	Nov =	*11 + PLC 2 =	4 IMC
Dec =	3 + PLC 1 =	4 IMC	Dec =	3 + PLC 2 =	5 IMC

PLC of 3   PLC of 4

Jan =	1 + PLC 3 =	4 IMC**	Jan =	1 + PLC 4 =	5 IMC**
Feb =	2 + PLC 3 =	5 IMC	Feb =	2 + PLC 4 =	6 IMC
Mar =	3 + PLC 3 =	6 IMC	Mar =	3 + PLC 4 =	7 IMC
Apr =	4 + PLC 3 =	7 IMC	Apr =	4 + PLC 4 =	8 IMC
May =	5 + PLC 3 =	8 IMC	May =	5 + PLC 4 =	9 IMC
Jun =	6 + PLC 3 =	9 IMC	Jun =	6 + PLC 4 =	1 IMC
Jul =	7 + PLC 3 =	1 IMC	Jul =	7 + PLC 4 =	*11 IMC
Aug =	8 + PLC 3 =	*11 IMC	Aug =	8 + PLC 4 =	3 IMC
Sep =	9 + PLC 3 =	3 IMC**	Sep =	9 + PLC 4 =	4 IMC**
Oct =	1 + PLC 3 =	4 IMC**	Oct =	1 + PLC 4 =	5 IMC**
Nov =	*11 + PLC 3 =	5 IMC	Nov =	*11 + PLC 4 =	6 IMC
Dec =	3 + PLC 3 =	6 IMC	Dec =	3 + PLC 4 =	7 IMC

PLC of 5   PLC of 6

Jan =	1 + PLC 5 =	6 IMC**	Jan =	1 + PLC 6 =	7 IMC**
Feb =	2 + PLC 5 =	7 IMC	Feb =	2 + PLC 6 =	8 IMC
Mar =	3 + PLC 5 =	8 IMC	Mar =	3 + PLC 6 =	9 IMC
Apr =	4 + PLC 5 =	9 IMC	Apr =	4 + PLC 6 =	1 IMC
May =	5 + PLC 5 =	1 IMC	May =	5 + PLC 6 =	*11 IMC
Jun =	6 + PLC 5 =	*11 IMC	Jun =	6 + PLC 6 =	3 IMC
Jul =	7 + PLC 5 =	3 IMC	Jul =	7 + PLC 6 =	4 IMC
Aug =	8 + PLC 5 =	4 IMC	Aug =	8 + PLC 6 =	5 IMC
Sep =	9 + PLC 5 =	5 IMC**	Sep =	9 + PLC 6 =	6 IMC**
Oct =	1 + PLC 5 =	6 IMC**	Oct =	1 + PLC 6 =	7 IMC**

Nov =	*11 + PLC 5 =	7 IMC	Nov =	*11 + PLC 6 =	8 IMC
Dec =	3 + PLC 5 =	8 IMC	Dec =	3 + PLC 6 =	9 IMC

PLC of 7   PLC of 8

Jan =	1 + PLC 7 =	8 IMC**	**Jan** =	1 + PLC 8 =	9 IMC**
Feb =	2 + PLC 7 =	9 IMC	Feb =	2 + PLC 8 =	1 IMC
Mar =	3 + PLC 7 =	1 IMC	Mar =	3 + PLC 8 =	*11 IMC
Apr =	4 + PLC 7 =	*11 IMC	Apr =	4 + PLC 8 =	3 IMC
May =	5 + PLC 7 =	3 IMC	May =	5 + PLC 8 =	4 IMC
Jun =	6 + PLC 7 =	4 IMC	Jun =	6 + PLC 8 =	5 IMC
Jul =	7 + PLC 7 =	5 IMC	Jul =	7 + PLC 8 =	6 IMC
Aug =	8 + PLC 7 =	6 IMC	Aug =	8 + PLC 8 =	7 IMC
Sep =	9 + PLC 7 =	7 IMC**	**Sep** =	9 + PLC 8 =	8 IMC**
Oct =	1 + PLC 7 =	8 IMC**	**Oct** =	1 + PLC 8 =	9 IMC**
Nov =	*11 + PLC 7 =	9 IMC	Nov =	*11 + PLC 8 =	1 IMC
Dec =	3 + PLC 7 =	1 IMC	Dec =	3 + PLC 8 =	*11 IMC

PLC of 9   PLC of *11

Jan =	1 + PLC 9 =	1 IMC**	**Jan** =	1 + PLC *11 =	3 IMC**
Feb =	2 + PLC 9 =	*11 IMC	Feb =	2 + PLC *11 =	4 IMC
Mar =	3 + PLC 9 =	3 IMC	Mar =	3 + PLC *11 =	5 IMC
Apr =	4 + PLC 9 =	4 IMC	Apr =	4 + PLC *11 =	6 IMC
May =	5 + PLC 9 =	5 IMC	May =	5 + PLC *11 =	7 IMC
Jun =	6 + PLC 9 =	6 IMC	May =	6 + PLC *11 =	8 IMC
Jul =	7 + PLC 9 =	7 IMC	Jul =	7 + PLC *11 =	9 IMC
Aug =	8 + PLC 9 =	8 IMC	Aug =	8 + PLC *11 =	1 IMC
Sep =	9 + PLC 9 =	9 IMC**	**Sep** =	9 + PLC *11 =	2 IMC**
Oct =	1 + PLC 9 =	1 IMC**	**Oct** =	1 + PLC *11 =	3 IMC**
Nov =	*11 + PLC 9 =	2 IMC	Nov =	*11 + PLC *11 =	*22 IMC
Dec =	3 + PLC 9 =	3 IMC	Dec =	3 + PLC *11 =	5 IMC

PLC of *22   PLC of *33

Jan =	1 + PLC *22 =	5 IMC**	**Jan** =	1 + PLC *33 =	7 IMC**
Feb =	2 + PLC *22 =	6 IMC	Feb =	2 + PLC *33 =	8 IMC
Mar =	3 + PLC *22 =	7 IMC	Mar =	3 + PLC *33 =	9 IMC

Apr =	4 + PLC *22 =	8 IMC	Apr =	4 + PLC *33 =	1 IMC
May =	5 + PLC *22 =	9 IMC	May =	5 + PLC *33 =	*11 IMC
Jun =	6 + PLC *22 =	1 IMC	Jun =	6 + PLC *33 =	3 IMC
Jul =	7 + PLC *22 =	*11 IMC	Jul =	7 + PLC *33 =	4 IMC
Aug =	8 + PLC *22 =	3 IMC	Aug =	8 + PLC *33 =	5 IMC
Sep =	9 + PLC *22 =	4 IMC**	**Sep** =	9 + PLC *33 =	6 IMC**
Oct =	1 + PLC *22 =	5 IMC**	Oct =	1 + PLC *33 =	7 IMC**
Nov =	*11 + PLC *22 =	*33 IMC	Nov =	*11 + PLC *33 =	8 IMC
Dec =	3 + PLC *22 =	7 IMC	Dec =	3 + PLC *33 =	9 IMC

TRANSITION BIRTHDAY

Birthdays falling within the period from OCTOBER 1 through JANUARY 7 are considered TRANSITION BIRTHDAYS (TB). People with Transition Birthdays experience an ADDITIONAL CYCLE CHANGE. There is a karmic connotation to these birthdays. The changing of Cycles assists in formulating the esoteric structure required to accomplish the Original Plan. The structure of the Natal Chart becomes somewhat more complex.

Transition Cycle

TB people undergo a TRANSITION CYCLE on the birthday which remains with them THROUGH JANUARY 7. A TB is *not* a negative situation! It is a mystical change of Cycles to accommodate the needs of the individual. Its impact is felt *immediately* on the actual birthday. This new Cycle, the Transition Cycle, operates at 100 percent effectiveness, according to the Rootings, and continues this way through January 7. On January 8 the person will once again receive the full impact of the new PLC as the Transition Cycle diminishes.

The journey of a soul through any one calendar year has its ups and downs, its highs and lows. Now let's follow the pattern of events of a typical TB person.

January

Like everyone else, the TB person will feel the vibratory force of the Karmic Sun. The difference is that "Mr. TB" will be very intensely focused during the first seven days of the year. Resolutions will be made, memories relived and his general attitude will be quite philosophical.

On January 8, Mr. TB is suddenly confronted with a new and vibrant PLC. The impact is felt immediately. Usually he will enjoy this new vibratory field of expression—it appears to release him from the condensed energy encapsulated in the first seven days of January.

September

From his new PLC received on January 8 and lasting through August 31, Mr. TB experiences his IMCs in the same vibratory sequence as everyone else. But now, beginning on September 1, he must concentrate on the merging of Cycles and be certain that he is satisfied with his progress to date. He has the entire month of September to reflect upon and complete what he must accomplish.

October

With October 1 comes the Monitor Month, bringing a preview of next year's vibratory forces. Like everyone else, Mr. TB should project his attention toward the future and plan accordingly. Now, let's give Mr. TB his Transition Birthday and current PLC:

BIRTHDAY	PLC
November 21	4

November

On his exact birthday, Mr. TB goes into his Transition Cycle, which is computed like this:

CURRENT PLC   =   4
INCOMING PLC   =   5
TRANSITION CYCLE   =   9

Nature of Essence

Our next step is to analyze the NATURE OF ESSENCE (NE) of Mr. TB's Transition Cycle. This is the term used to indicate the substance of the energies that form his Transition Cycle of NINE.

The Nature of Essence for Mr. TB is the FOUR and the FIVE. In order to utilize this information properly, we must next determine the actual *percentage of each number* as it relates to Mr. TB's birthday.

THE TRANSITION GRID

The percentage of each current and incoming PLC for all Transition Birthdays (October 1 through January 7) are given in a handy table called the TRANSITION GRID (see page 57). Using this table, you can quickly determine the correct percentages to be applied to any TB. For example, with Mr. TB's birthday of November 21, look at the line of numbers following "November." When you come to 21, the number directly beneath it will be the percentage of the CURRENT PLC (4) to be used, which is 48 percent. Directly beneath that, you will find the percentage of the INCOMING PLC (5) to be used, which is 52 percent. (Note: In the interests of consistency, but perhaps at the expense of clarity, I have used Peter's PLCs [8 and 9] on the Grid, but the percentages remain the same for *all* PLCs.)

So, having consulted the Transition Grid, you now have the exact percentages which comprise the Nature of Essence of Mr. TB's Transition Cycle of NINE:

48% of the FOUR

52% of the FIVE

100%

Mr. TB, therefore, should activate his new Transition Cycle of NINE using the above degrees of the FOUR and FIVE. This procedure

Transition Grid for 1988:   PLC of 8 going into a PLC of 9.   Peter Paul Connolly.

October

	1	2	3	4	5	6	7	8	9	10	11	12	13	14	15	16	17	18	19	20	21	22	23	24	25	26	27	28	29	30	31
PLC 8 %	99	98	97	96	95	94	93	92	91	90	89	88	87	86	85	84	83	82	81	80	79	78	77	76	75	74	73	72	71	70	69
PLC 9 %	1	2	3	4	5	6	7	8	9	10	11	12	13	14	15	16	17	18	19	20	21	22	23	24	25	26	27	28	29	30	31

November

	1	2	3	4	5	6	7	8	9	10	11	12	13	14	15	16	17	18	19	20	21	22	23	24	25	26	27	28	29	30
PLC 8 %	68	67	66	65	64	63	62	61	60	59	58	57	56	55	54	53	52	51	50	49	48	47	46	45	44	43	42	41	40	39
PLC 9 %	32	33	34	35	36	37	38	39	40	41	42	43	44	45	46	47	48	49	50	51	52	53	54	55	56	57	58	59	60	61

December

	1	2	3	4	5	6	7	8	9	10	11	12	13	14	15	16	17	18	19	20	21	22	23	24	25	26	27	28	29	30	31
PLC 8 %	38	37	36	35	34	33	32	31	30	29	28	27	26	25	24	23	22	21	20	19	18	17	16	15	14	13	12	11	10	9	8
PLC 9 %	62	63	64	65	66	67	68	69	70	71	72	73	74	75	76	77	78	79	80	81	82	83	84	85	86	87	88	89	90	91	92

January

	1	2	3	4	5	6	7	8
PLC 8 %	7	6	5	4	3	2	1	
PLC 9 %	93	94	95	96	97	98	99	100%

January 1st through 7th is the 7 Day Mystic Birth Cycle:

Personal Life Cycle ends on day 99 = 18 = 9 = Complete Cycle of Man:

January 8th = 100% of new Personal Life Cycle 9.

January 8th through September 30th through September 30th Year? PLC is stabilized.

{ Birthdays from January 8th through September 30th {impact of PLC energy on Birthday.

{ Birthdays from October 1st through January 7th are Transition Birthdays.

should bring him directly to his desired goals; it is the direct route to his continuing success. He should first recognize the needs of the NINE; the means to achieve those needs lie in the two separate numbers and their percentages, which comprise the Nature of Essence.

From his birthday on November 21 through January 7, the Transition Cycle of NINE with its Nature of Essence for the FOUR and FIVE will be functioning at 100 percent efficiency.

The Transition Grid shows a simple structure of increasing and decreasing numerical vibrations for each of the four Transition months (October through January). The number of the Transition Cycle is always obtained by adding together the numbers of the current and incoming PLCs.

OTHER TRANSITION BIRTHDAYS

Understanding this rather complex procedure is of vital importance to the Consultant, as you are bound to run into many clients whose birthdays fall within the Transition Months. So, to make sure you understand how this business works, here are some further examples of TBs for you to practice on:

1.	CURRENT PLC	INCOMING PLC	BIRTHDAY
	1	2	October 14

ONE + TWO = TRANSITION CYCLE OF THREE. The Nature of Essence lies in the ONE and the TWO. Consulting the Transition Grid, you can see that on the birthday, the Transition Cycle of THREE must be implemented as follows:

86% of the ONE

14% of the TWO

An in-depth interpretation of this formula would require a study of the completed Natal Chart, which would show WHY and in WHICH AREAS the Nature of Essence should be used. This client has just experienced the impact of the duplication of PLC ONE with IMC ONE during September. Regardless of the effects of this merging, the Nature of Essence requires a considerable amount of energy to be channelled through the ONE—86 percent, to be exact. It would appear that with the minimum degrees of only 14 percent the client has cooperated and negotiated with others sufficiently at this point. Apparently it merely requires that another person become involved in tying up the ends of the present situation to complete the 14 percent. As for the THREE, it requires a personal outward expression of individual activity. This client needs to demonstrate his talents and in general expose the issue that has been energized by his individuality during the year. The high percentage of the ONE still to be used will ignite the need of the THREE to be expressed fully during the period from his birthday through January 7.

	CURRENT PLC	INCOMING PLC	BIRTHDAY
2.	2	3	November 2
3.	3	4	November 23
4.	4	5	October 19
5.	5	6	December 4
6.	6	7	December 23
7.	7	8	October 29

Determine the Transition Cycles and Natures of Essence for the above examples. Now answer the following questions for each example:

1. After observing the current PLC and how it has been administered, how do you feel the person can best make use of his Transition Cycle?

2. What is the balance of energies contained within the Nature of Essence? In what way will the energies of each Cycle contribute to the new Transition Cycle?

3. When will the energy from the Transition Cycle subside?

4. When will the new PLC become activated?

5. What are the beginning and ending dates of the Mystic Birth Cycle (MBC)?

6. How can you use the knowledge of the Transition Birthday Cycle for your client's benefit?

7. How quickly is the impact of these inner Cycles felt?

8. Describe the esoteric energy that dominates January. What is the energy called?

TRANSITION MYSTIC CYCLE

This unique Transition Period, consisting of Cycles within Cycles, combines into one mystical period of changing events called the TRANSITION MYSTIC CYCLE (TMC). Here's how it relates to the various days and months of the Transition Period:

OCTOBER = 31 DAYS (TMC begins October 1)

NOVEMBER = 30 DAYS

DECEMBER = 31 DAYS (TMC ends December 31)

SUBTOTAL = 92 DAYS = *11 TMC Period

ADD = 7 DAYS = MYSTIC BIRTH CYCLE (January 1–7)

TOTAL = 99 DAYS = 18 = 9 (The Number of the Completion of Man)

If you look at the Transition Grid, you will see how the 92 days of the TMC plus the seven days of the MBC are divided into degrees from October 1 until the Esoteric New Year of January 8. On this day *everyone* experiences their new PLC at a full 100 percent, whether they have Transition Birthdays or not.

All birthdays follow the daily degree formula throughout Transition until those with TBs reach their birthdays. They follow the information given specifically for them in the previous section. For those with birthdays from January 8 through September 30, you will have a gradual change of Cycles, commencing October 1. As the Transition Grid shows, each day of the Transition Period you will

1. LOSE ONE DEGREE OF THE CURRENT PERSONAL LIFE CYCLE

2. GAIN ONE DEGREE OF THE INCOMING PERSONAL LIFE CYCLE.

This method of losing and gaining degrees arrives at a balanced mid-point on NOVEMBER 19. On this day you experience exactly 50 percent of BOTH PLCs. Decisions can go either way at this point. It's not the best day to make important decisions, for there may be a conflict between the vibratory frequencies of each Cycle, since they are now of equal intensity. However, if the two Cycles are complementary to each other, there should be no trouble.

The importance of SEPTEMBER, with its solidified IMC and PLC, should now become apparent to you. After this input of crystallized energies, October introduces the reduction of daily degrees of the current PLC. If a particular goal needs to be achieved during the current year, and if by September it hasn't gotten off the ground, it would be wise to motivate yourself to make the effort of dealing with this situation during September, before October arrives.

However, I have known clients who experienced great difficulties in arriving at serious decisions. September came and went and still they hadn't solved their problem. But as the changing Cycles became more powerful, they found the strength to deal with the situation, because the incoming Cycle released the grip of the current Cycle, allowing them more freedom of thought and action.

The lesson here is to tune into *both* Cycles. Consider what your goals are, then estimate the degree of strength necessary to achieve them, relative to the energies of both the current and incoming PLCs.

Statistics have shown that during DECEMBER, the last full month of Transition, many depressing situations can arise. Suicides are frequent at this time, for many are depressed due to lack of income, inability to be with their families, sorrow for a deceased loved one, etc. We tend to overlook these facts as we are caught up in the holiday festivities of Chanukkah and Christmas. These and other holy days during this period originated from ancient feast days fixed, I believe, according to the esoteric pattern of vibrations that were experienced on those days. The ancients planned these festive days in a deliberate attempt to lift people's spirits and raise them out of themselves a bit, thus relieving the pressures and frustrations of their Cycles.

MYSTIC BIRTH CYCLE

It's easy to overlook the short Cycle called the MYSTIC BIRTH CYCLE (MBC) that occurs from JANUARY 1 through JANUARY 7.

But it is extremely important in improving the changeover of Cycles, for it is the *birth channel* for the incoming PLC.

Here's how this period usually breaks down in our lives:

JANUARY 1   New Year festivities, parties, ball games.

JANUARY 2   Aftermath of parties, returning home, cleaning up, preparing for the reality of the new year.

JANUARY 3   A day of recuperating, making swift adjustments, getting back into the daily routines, going back to work.

JANUARY 4,5,6,7   These days have a strange feeling: our thoughts dwell on the year ahead; often we suffer remorse for the year that is gone.

Many people unfortunately experience the MBC, but without any knowledge of how to handle the feelings and events it generates.

During the Mystic Birth Cycle, a period of seven days, the new PLC is being born. Mental, spiritual and physical levels should all be in balance at this time in order for the incoming Cycle to produce its optimum effect. This should be a time of cleansing and releasing old worn-out concepts, everything that is not conducive to new life and energy. Hesitation and contemplation should be well behind you at this time; any lingering signs of resistance or reluctance should be overcome. Use the MBC to prepare for the new and vibrant energies that are coming to help you achieve your purpose. The MBC is offering you a new start, a new direction and a new approach. New stamina, new ideas, a NEW YOU are created on your ESOTERIC NEW YEAR.

ESOTERIC SEED DAY

The ESOTERIC SEED is the number of the Original Plan. Contained within this vibration is everything the soul requires to experience true happiness. Having this knowledge can prevent missed opportunities and when used deliberately, can open wide vistas of new possibilities.

To compute your ESOTERIC SEED DAY (ESD), first take the number of your OP, which you have already obtained.[1] In Peter's case, this number is a TWO, calculated as follows:

PETER'S BIRTHDAY:	MONTH = AUGUST	=	8
	DAY	=	1
	YEAR	=	1964
	TOTAL	=	1973 = 20 = 2 OP

Therefore, ANY DAY in ANY MONTH in ANY YEAR that has a WORLD DAY CYCLE (WDC) of TWO or *11 will be an ESOTERIC SEED DAY for Peter. (Note that the EMVs [*11, *22, *33] are *not* reduced to a single digit in calculating the ESD. A Master Number increases the energy of the ESD.

World Day Cycle

The second part of this calculation is finding the WORLD DAY CYCLE (WDC) which corresponds to the number of the OP. This is done as follows:

YEAR (CHRIST CYCLE)[2] =	1988	= 26 =	8
MONTH	JANUARY	=	1
DAY	2	=	2
TOTAL		= *11 =	*11 ESD on 1/2/88

Therefore, January 2, is the *first* ESD for Peter in 1988. Using this formula, you can calculate all the ESDs for yourself for the entire year. Here, for example, are all of Peter's ESDs for the Month of January 1988:

JANUARY 2 = *11 (Additional EMV energy indicates that this ESD may have special qualities.)

JANUARY 11 = 2 (Master Number *11 is not reduced.)

JANUARY 20 = *11

JANUARY 29 = *11

[1]See: Vol. I, Chapter 11, p. 119.
[2]See: Vol. I, Chapter 8, pp. 46–47.

So Peter has a total of FOUR ESDs in January which contain THREE Master Vibrations of *11. Since a Master Number increases the energy of the ESD, it appears that January could be very special for Peter, bringing him the opportunity to tune into ideas and activities relating to his Original Plan.

Individual Day Cycle

Next, we should consider the INDIVIDUAL DAY CYCLE (IDC)[3] and see how this Aspect correlates with the ESD. Once again we will use Peter's Chart as an example. We have already determined his ESDs for January 1988. Now when we compare them with his IDCs, we discover something unusual:

ESOTERIC SEED DAYS			INDIVIDUAL DAY CYCLE		
JANUARY 2	=	*11	JANUARY 2	=	*11
JANUARY 11	=	2	JANUARY 11	=	2
JANUARY 20	=	*11	JANUARY 20	=	*11
JANUARY 29	=	*11	JANUARY 29	=	*11

Peter's IDCs are *identical* to his ESDs! This is because his OP is *always* identical to the CHRIST CYCLE (CC) for the year of his birth:

$$OP = 2 \qquad 1964 = 20 = 2 \ CC$$

This duplication only occurs when a person's CC number (birth year number) and OP number are the same. Study the following examples to get a clearer picture of how this works.

NAME	YEAR OF BIRTH	CHRIST CYCLE	ORIGINAL PLAN
Deborah	1954	1	7
Catherine	1955	2	3
Benedict	1956	3	5
Louise	1957	*22	6
Jonathan	1959	6	3
Oliver	1978	SEVEN	SEVEN

[3]See: Vol. I, Chapter 11, pp. 167–168.

DEBORAH

Esoteric Seed Days	Individual Day Cycle
JANUARY 7 = 7	JANUARY 7 = 3
JANUARY 16 = 7	JANUARY 16 = 3
JANUARY 25 = 7	JANUARY 25 = 3

CATHERINE

JANUARY 3 = 3	JANUARY 3 = 4
JANUARY 12 = 3	JANUARY 12 = *22
JANUARY 21 = 3	JANUARY 21 = 4

BENEDICT

JANUARY 5 = 5	JANUARY 5 = 7
JANUARY 14 = 5	JANUARY 14 = 7
JANUARY 23 = 5	JANUARY 23 = 7

LOUISE

JANUARY 6 = 6	JANUARY 6 = 8
JANUARY 15 = 6	JANUARY 15 = 8
JANUARY 24 = 6	JANUARY 24 = 8

JONATHAN

JANUARY 3 = 3	JANUARY 3 = 9
JANUARY 12 = 3	JANUARY 12 = 9
JANUARY 21 = 3	JANUARY 21 = 9
JANUARY 30 = 3	JANUARY 30 = 9

OLIVER

JANUARY 7 = 7	JANUARY 7 = 7
JANUARY 16 = 7	JANUARY 16 = 7
JANUARY 25 = 7	JANUARY 25 = 7

In the last example, you can see that, like Peter, Oliver's ESDs are identical to his IDCs. This is because, like Peter, his Original Plan is identical to the Christ Cycle of the year he was born. This identical frequency becomes a FIXED ASPECT, and each year both Peter and Oliver will undergo the same sequence.

The effects of this intensification of energy through duplication can be seen in the need to accomplish a specific goal. This goal, of course, is the Original Plan. People born within the rhythm of the Christ Cycle are always inwardly striving to achieve something and will show little or no interest in things that do not contribute to that achievement. Like a horse with blinders, they keep their eyes on the finishing post and are not easily distracted. Whether the race is easy or difficult, their attitude toward winning seldom changes.

Now let's analyze our six examples a little further:

DEBORAH: ESD = 7   IDC = 3

Deborah has the opportunity to express openly what she feels inside. The ESD of 7 can find its outlet through the IDCs of 3.

CATHERINE: ESD = 3   IDC = 4

January will bring days of solid grounding to Catherine, days when she can present her ideas and plans in a calm, orderly manner.

BENEDICT: ESD = 5   IDC = 7

Benedict's IDCs will have a soothing effect; they will be good days to think things over. He will feel right spending time alone.

LOUISE: ESD = 6   IDC = 8

This combination shows that Louise should launch any plans or ideas she has been formulating.

JONATHAN: ESD = 3   IDC = 9

This is a great month for Jonathan to look toward the future. Extended vision and future activities should be his focus during this month.

OLIVER: ESD = 7   IDC = 7

This young man of ten years may have quite a serious month in January. On his special days he may become caught up in interesting new projects. He should enjoy being alone. He could discover a new talent in himself and feel very satisfied with it.

As a Consultant, you should check the ESDs before your client arrives. This will help you achive the rapport you need to make him feel more in tune and focused.

The ESD gives additional power to the DAY in relation to the ORIGINAL PLAN. The numerical vibration of the ESD is focused directly onto the OP, expanding its potential and giving added insight into its purpose.

In conclusion, here are four things to remember when analyzing ESD/IDC relationships:

1. The ESD expands the purpose of the Original Plan.

2. The IDC shows you the type of day and the vibratory frequency you may expect from it.

3. By understanding the vibration of the day, you can exercise the intent contained within the Original Plan.

4. On this day you feel more in tune with your own identity. You are more confident and outgoing in your ideas and plans. The vibrations are vitalized with true intent. Others will be attracted to this energy and will be more eager to listen and cooperate with you. This receptivity can also enhance the purpose of the Original Plan.

DAILY VIBRATIONAL LEVEL

In working further with the IDC, you'll find that it can give you the numerical "temperature" of any specific day you choose to delineate. You'll usually want to refer to this information when you have a particularly important day ahead, one with significant circumstances or obligations.

If time is a factor, then you must learn to work with certain periods of time—the DAILY VIBRATIONAL LEVEL (DVL) of the IDC. For example, in working with an IDC of FOUR followed by an IDC of FIVE (use ONE GRAPH SQUARE to represent EACH HOUR):

1. The NEW INCOMING IDC of 4 comes in at 3:00 A.M.

2. The vibratory level of IDC 4 remains constant for TWELVE HOURS: 3:00 A.M.–3:00 P.M.

3. During the following SIX HOURS, the energies gradually subside, reaching their lowest point at 9:00 P.M.: 3:00 P.M.–9:00 P.M.

4. During the next SIX-HOUR period, the INCOMING IDC 5 begins to fuse with the outgoing energy of IDC 4: 9:00 P.M.–3:00 A.M.

5. The INCOMING IDC of 5 becomes dominant at 3:00 A.M.

So you can see that during any period of TWENTY-FOUR HOURS, the DVL ebbs and flows like this:

3:00 A.M.	= New IDC comes in
3:00 A.M.–3:00 P.M.	= Height of IDC energy sustained
3:00 P.M.–9:00 P.M.	= Gradual decline of IDC
9:00 P.M.	= Transition of IDC
9:00 P.M.–3:00 A.M.	= Old IDC wanes, new IDC gains strength

EXACT KARMIC ALIGNMENT

Once every NINE YEARS you experience the EXACT KARMIC ALIGNMENT (EKA). At this time the soul is in true alignment with the ORIGINAL KARMIC INTENTION. The energies and opportunities available on this one day can establish a deep understanding of personal goals and the desired level of success.

The EKA occurs on the PHYSICAL BIRTHDAY (PB) during the PERSONAL LIFE CYCLE that coincides with the ORIGINAL PLAN. For example, here are the nine-year periods in Peter's Chart:

EKA YEAR	CHRIST CYCLE	ORIGINAL PLAN	PERSONAL LIFE CYCLE
1964 (Physical Birthday)	2	2	2
ADD NINE YEARS			
1973	2	2	2
ADD NINE YEARS			
1982	2	2	2
ADD NINE YEARS			
1991 (Next EKA Year)	2	2	2

Note: When delineating the EKA, if any EMVs are obtained (*11, *22, *33), they are reduced to 2, 4 and 6 respectively.

It's interesting to go back to your past EKA days. Try to recall what was happening on those particular birthdays. If you chose to ignore the advantages they brought, your memories may be full of regret. But if you have made good use of these special energies, you will find that your past EKA days were responsible for many wonderful events in your life—events which made a tremendous difference in some way.

VERTEX

At this point we must now consider the fusing of energies of numerical vibrations. Volume I gives various interpretations for each number (Chapters 5 and 10, pp. 28, 29, 89–98); now let's go beyond this point and consider the effects of the VERTEX (VX) when two consecutive numbers merge.

This Aspect should not be ignored on any Level of inquiry or delineation. With sufficient research, you may discover several periods of advantage during which your client can benefit from the peaking energies at the Vertex. The combined influence of certain numbers can be quite beneficial to some, while others may have the opposite reaction, so it behooves you to learn to recognize the vibratory needs of each client by diligent and careful study and updating of his Chart.

ALL ASPECTS, LEVELS AND CYCLES have a Vertex; here is an esoteric view of the inner workings of the Chart. Cycles within Cycles open and fuse into one another, all governed by their own individual timing processes. Like the inner workings of the human body, the esoteric pattern of numerical Cycles is constantly functioning. To succeed and prosper according to your karmic destiny, you need to attune and align yourself exactly with these mysterious energy patterns which affect your Original Plan in this life.

The Vertex is the merging and fusing of ANY TWO NUMBERS, at the point of impact and *before* the incoming Cycle commences its influence. This mysterious moment in time extends a profound effect prior to the influence of the new Cycle.

At the time of the Vertex there is a surge of energy as the incoming vibrations combine with the outgoing ones. You experience a vibratory level entirely different from any numerical force you know! There is *no* numerical identification for the vibratory level of the Vertex, because it is composed of two different numerical levels.

For example, when a ONE converges with a TWO, within a limited time you will experience a totally different numerical energy which is neither the frequency of the ONE nor the TWO, but a *combination* of both in an esoteric interpretation whose origin goes back to the Cabalistic teachings of the Ancient Masters.

Everyone must receive their own vibratory level of any one number before they respond to its force. Like certain kinds of foods, every individual has an "appetite" for certain amounts of various numerical frequencies. Some people have a great appetite for the Vertex energy; others dislike it, and still others thrive on only an occasional Vertex.

You are now in an area of numerical vibratory levels that is not usually recognized or considered. Your initial research into this advanced area should be focused on your own Chart. You may find that in early childhood you had a large appetite for Vertex energy; or you may discover that you were "allergic" to it. However, since then your appetite may have changed, so this area should be explored by careful research into your Chart.

If for example you find that the Vertex energy upsets you, then you would have to recognize that it is evident in all your Aspects and in the INTERCHANGE OF CYCLES. If you discover that you are so acutely attuned to the Vertex that you react each month as your outgoing IMC merges with your incoming IMC, you may find that you are experiencing this reaction as a physical situation in your life. I feel that biorhythms, which have received much attention lately, are in fact the result of numerical inner Cycles and Aspects converging in Vertex energy.

Some people are so sensitive to Vertex energy that they react to it even on a *daily* basis! This is apparent if the client shows a reaction about 9:00 P.M. each evening. The pattern often goes like this:

1. High energy in the day; best work completed by 3:00 P.M.

2. Lack of energy—in bed or resting by 9:00 P.M.

3. Decisions made earlier in the day appear to be less firm or need adjustment from 9:00 P.M. on.

4. During sleep, vivid dreams occur, some being predictive.

About fifteen years ago I did extensive research on these patterns of sensitivity which confirmed my Vertex theory. Another interesting result of this research was the discovery that these reactions can vary from day to day. Changes occur which cause a person to be vulnerable or allergic to Vertex energy. These changes seem to be rooted in the person's actual sensitivity to the energy patterns of others. Some respond well and are attracted to other people's vibrations; some tend to avoid them.

So you can see that this level of sensitivity goes beyond your own Natal Aspects and Cycles: you can be influenced by those of others! Taking this one step further, I then found that these supersensitive people usually have great psychic potential, which they may or may not be aware of. This level of sensitivity may be explored by analyzing the reaction of their merging Cycles on any Aspect or Cycle change.

The Vertex is only one limited example of the potential of inner vibratory sequences that cannot be identified through normal numerical procedures. This advanced study is rooted in the ancient Cabalistic teachings. The Cabalistic scholar is continually striving to obtain knowledge from the infinite origin. He reaches a point of understanding and then a point of silence. Then it becomes his duty to determine the need for this wisdom and how to release it for the greatest benefit of mankind.

In conclusion, here are some procedures to explore in working with the Vertex energy in relation to the Natal Chart:

1. Recognize the DOMINANT numbers on the O Level.

2. Determine HOW the client USES these dominant vibrations.

3. Recognize WHEN decisions are instigated.

4. Determine WHETHER the client ACTS WELL within the Aspects or Cycles.

5. Determine the TIMES when the client is most productive and positive.

6. Determine the VERTEX choices of the client.

Now, as we proceed to examine the remaining advanced Aspects of the Transition Period, I will introduce you to the NATAL TRANSITION WHEEL.

CHAPTER 5

THE NATAL TRANSITION WHEEL

The NATAL TRANSITION WHEEL (NTW) and its various allied Aspects have been carefully formulated out of my many years of Cabalistic research and study. This information has not been published previously, and it is my hope that you will be among the first to find it helpful in your studies of advanced Gnothology. Once you learn the rhythm of the Wheel and all its ramifications, you'll understand clearly just *how* and *when* the various Cycles work. You will come to understand the timing involved and learn to recognize the periods of peak activity throughout each year.

Because of the precision of the Transition Wheel, you will be able to sharpen your forecasting abilities and provide your clients with greater accuracy as a Consultant. Being exact is exciting and rewarding—it takes extra effort but is well worth it.

INDEX OF TRANSITION ASPECTS

The following are the Aspects we will be dealing with next. Like the ten in the preceding chapter, all seven of these can be classified as SOURCE: BIRTH and SECTION: PARTURITIVE.

CODE   TITLE

1. NTW   Natal Transition Wheel

2. EB   Esoteric Birthday

3. TBC   Transition Bridge Cycle

	CODE	TITLE
4.	TJ	Transition Juncture
5.	TI	Transition Impediment
6.	BT	Balancing Tool
7.	NTT	Natal Transition Table[1]

ESOTERIC BIRTHDAY

The ESOTERIC BIRTHDAY (EB), as opposed to the regular Physical Birthday (PB), occurs FOUR MONTHS PRIOR to the actual date of birth. On this date the planetary aspects and vibrational levels for the Physical Birth are structured. At this time the soul becomes aware of its physical heritage; the karmic destiny is complete and waiting to be expressed in a new life. During this period the Esoteric Body is preparing for the complete merging of your ESOTERIC and PHYSICAL SELF in the fetus. The time slot during the pregnancy is the fifth month, usually after the mother has felt the first physical movements in the womb. The Ancients called this event the "Quickening."

Therefore, Peter, having been born August 1, 1964, experienced his EB on APRIL 1, 1964 (see NTW Chart on p. 75). On this exact date new ideas flooded into his level of consciousness.

What actually happens is that the higher consciousness is able to penetrate the level of the subconscious, which in turn is felt on the normal conscious level. Sometimes deep and meaningful dreams occur on this date each year. You may notice sudden changes in people's behavior patterns, particularly in women. Many people make major decisions regarding their needs on their Esoteric Birthday and in so doing, may appear to act hastily. The impact of the EB sometimes appears to affect the normal thinking process, producing an impression of impulsiveness, but in fact the decision made may very well be a wise and beneficial one.

Often excellent ideas spring from the EB Level, directing you toward your original karmic goals. Some people grasp these ideas and put them into action, but others resist the energy and continue to put their efforts into present situations that have evolved beyond their comprehension.

[1]The NTT will be discussed in a separate chapter, Chapter 6.

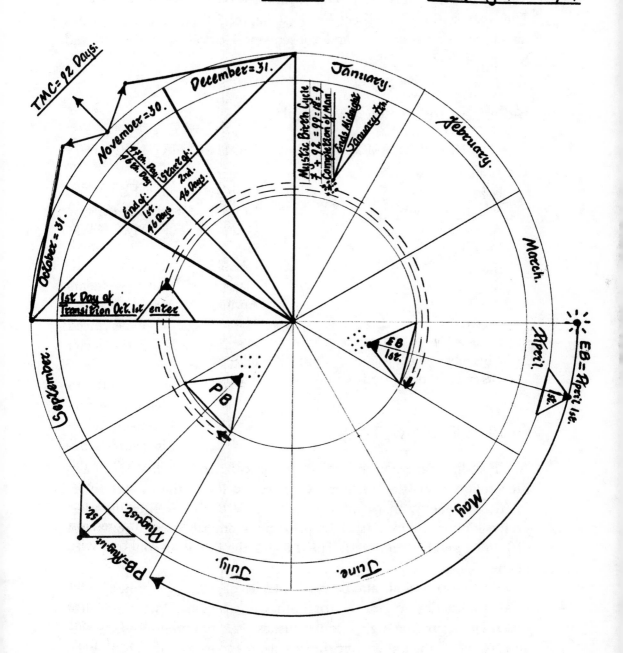

Natal Transition Wheel.

Peter Paul Connolly: Born August 1st 1964:

This particular Aspect is extremely interesting. Thought patterns are vivid and the reaction to the EB Level is one of the most exciting ways to improve and change your life situation. But if ignored or misused, the EB can cause despondency and lead to feelings of depression. The Stabilization Point (see: Vol. I, Chapter 10, pp. 100–104) brings into focus the possibilities and consequences of releasing the old and trying the new.

Esoteric Birthday Reference Table

PHYSICAL BIRTH MONTH	ESOTERIC BIRTH MONTH
January	September
February	October* (Note that the EB
March	November* Level is in the Tran-
April	December* sition Mystic Cycle.)
May	January
June	February
July	March
August	April
September	May
October* (Note that the date of	June
November* birth is in the Transi-	July
December* tion Mystic Cycle.)	August

Past-Life Therapy

Past-life regression through hypnosis can produce flashes of past-life situations. As the therapist regresses the client, the subject enters the field of energy that contains the Esoteric Birth Level. He may experience many quick flashes of previous memories, often appearing disjointed and disconnected. This I feel is the initial meeting with the Higher Self.

The subconscious and conscious levles of the mind cannot be activated until Physical Birth, for both work together in the physical body. However, the higher consciousness is held within the EB Level and retains all the knowledge, information and lessons that have been learned from previous lives *plus* the knowledge of lessons still to be learned.

During the client's regression, the conscious level gives way to the subconscious, which then exposes the higher consciousness. As the Higher Self knows well its own identity and purpose, it releases past-life memories into the conscious mind. This commences *first* by penetrating the SEED of karma which became active on the EB, four months prior to Physical Birth.

To fully understand and make use of past-life memories you must understand the route through the levels of consciousness. Upon reaching the Esoteric Seed the Higher Self opens its archives and reveals in a more coherent fashion the highlights of past lives.

Once the therapist has regressed the client to the higher level of consciousness, he will be able to then select certain vibratory frequencies and retrieve fixed vibratory patterns which reveal the esoteric memories in an encapsulated form. Beyond this point, the therapist must display great skill. He may wish to pursue a particular vibratory level which he considers favorable to his client. Through suggestion, he may help the client focus on a specific memory or sequence of memories without anxiety. If this is accomplished properly, the client can relax fully within that level and speak of certain events and relationships in that past life that have meaning in his present one. A good therapist can skillfully navigate his way through these levels to find the Esoteric Seed which has been structured four months prior to birth and which contains the higher consciousness. Then he can go beyond the Seed into more explicit detail wherever necessary.[2]

TRANSITION BRIDGE CYCLE

ONCE A YEAR, on the Esoteric Birthday, access to past-life memories becomes much easier. A simple but precise Gnothology Aspect can give you the Key.

The TRANSITION BRIDGE CYCLE (TBC) is a delineation which reveals and highlights past-life experiences and endeavors. It occurs only once a year, and each year the experiences will differ. This is because past-life experiences or relationships will always be in reference to what is occuring in your lifetime at *present*.

[2]For more information on past-life therapy, see: Dr. Bruce Goldberg, *Past Lives— Future Lives* (N. Hollywood, CA: Newcastle, 1982).

The Transition Bridge is crossed through a numerical formula which exposes us to events or emotional levels that pertain to past-life experiences considered by the Higher Self to be relevant to present-life activity. This can be achieved through meditation, or the information can come in a dream.

The number of days in Transition PRIOR to the Mystic Birth Cycle (MBC) is 92 DAYS. As you will recall, the MBC covers the period from January 1–7. Transition begins October 1 and ends December 31. This period of 92 days is divided into TWO PERIODS of 46 days each (see NTW Chart). As the 92 days DECREASE by ONE DEGREE DAILY of the present PERSONAL LIFE CYCLE, the incoming PLC is INCREASING by ONE DEGREE DAILY. The area of study here is the MID-POINT of this process.

1. FIRST 46 days of Transition = October 1–November 15.
2. On NOVEMBER 15 the OUTGOING PLC = 54%; the INCOMING PLC = 46%.
3. On NOVEMBER 16 the SECOND 46 days of Transition begin and the OUTGOING PLC = 53%; the INCOMING PLC = 47%.
4. On NOVEMBER 19 the INCOMING and OUTGOING PLCs are even at 50% each.

Note that this delineation of *degrees* encompasses the *entire* Transition Period, including the seven-day MBC in January. However, the number of *days* in the TMC is only 92 and ends on December 31.

Calculating the Transition Bridge Cycle

To arrive at the specific number for the TBC, which is an exacting Aspect, we need the following information:

1. TWO INDIVIDUAL DAY CYCLES—November 15 and 16 of the current year.
2. PHYSICAL BIRTHDAY with number of CURRENT PLC.
3. ESOTERIC BIRTHDAY with NEW PLC (4 months prior to PB).
4. CURRENT PLC on January 8 + MONTH and DATE.

Now we can set up our calculation, which will give us the number of the Transition Bridge Cycle. EMVs are *not* reduced for this calculation.

EXAMPLE ONE: PETER PAUL CONNOLLY

CURRENT IDC		PLC		MONTH		DAY				
November 15, 1987	=	7	+	*11	+	15			=	*33
November 16, 1987	=	7	+	*11	+	16	=	34	=	7
PB = August 1	=	8	+	8	+	1	=	17	=	8
EB = April 1	=	8	+	4	+	1	=	13	=	4
January 8, 1988	=	8	+	1	+	8	=	17	=	8
									60	= 6TBC 1988

So we arrive at a TBC number of SIX for Peter for the year 1988. Let's assume that this calculation was done in October 1987 in order to prepare Peter in advance, as his Esoteric Birthday will not be until April 1, 1988.

Looking at his Natal Chart we see that Peter does not have any SIXES on the required Aspects OSP, OPV, OEK and OP. When this occurs, the TBC number will become exceptionally important during the twelve months following the EB. With Peter, this means that from April 1, 1988 to April 1, 1989 the vibration of SIX will present an opportunity to complete a karmic desire through its use. Peter may meditate on the SIX and also use it as a tool consciously during the twelve-month period. In doing so, he will derive a level of karmic satisfaction which will bring him closer to his original Karmic Intention.

EXAMPLE TWO: EILEEN CONNOLLY

CURRENT IDC		PLC		MONTH		DAY				
November 15, 1987	=	6	+	*11	+	15	=	32	=	5
November 16, 1987	=	6	+	*11	+	16			=	*33
PB = May 3	=	7	+	5	+	3	=	15	=	6
EB = January 3	=	7	+	1	+	3			=	*11
January 8, 1988	=	7	+	1	+	8	=	16	=	7
									62	= 8TBC 1988

My personal example differs somewhat from Peter's. Although the two calculations were made at the same time, I will experience my Esoteric Birthday on January 3, 1988. My TBC number is EIGHT, and out of the four required Aspects, I find that I have an OSP of EIGHT.

Therefore, on my EB, January 3, I will meditate on the EIGHT with my focus on the ORIGINAL SOUL PRINT (see: Vol. I, Chapter 11, p. 109). Meditation on that day will open up my Karmic Intention with reference to the EIGHT and give me insight as to what I have to accomplish on the EIGHT vibratory level. When this information becomes known to me on the *conscious level*, then automatically all the other O Level Aspects will activate at the correct frequency. I should have the opportunity to consciously use the EIGHT to fulfill an original Karmic Intention. And it can also give me guidance in many other areas of life.

Utilizing the Transition Bridge Cycle

From these two examples you can sense the excitement of this Aspect. It will also seem exciting to your clients when you explain to them that this delineation presents a different vibratory force *each year* to be used in achieving their purposes and desires. The TBC has a special quality that is custom-made to correct your personal direction *every twelve months*. Each year this Aspect adapts to what is happening in your life at that time, providing insight, suggesting corrective measures and preventing you from repeating past mistakes.

The Bridge Cycle Procedure is excellent for anyone who suffers from uncertainty. Major decisions regarding educational matters, vocation, business, relationships, the location of a home and many other serious matters are governed by the TBC.

This Aspect is also ideal for younger clients as a means of giving them direction in life. Used on an annual basis, it will begin to develop a firm structural pattern in their lives. It's also helpful to look at your own Chart in relation to the TBC. Select a year that has strong memories for you and delineate the TBC for that year. This can give you deep insights into situations past and present. Testing these various Transition Aspects in your own Chart is an excellent way to improve your skill and understanding as a Consultant.

Keep in mind that life is not a contest! You are meant to achive your purpose and goals. Cross the Bridge Cycle each year and experience the confidence it gives, plus support for all your endeavors.

To sum up our study of the TBC, keep these principles in mind:

1. Meditation on the TBC number for each year will open the Esoteric Seed and release higher wisdom to fortify and correct your present life path.

2. Using the TBC number can shed light on past-life experiences that relate to your present life.

3. The intensity of this vibratory level is at its fullest potential *only* on the Esoteric Birthday.

4. When working with the degrees of the two 46-day periods of the TBC, remember to consider the VERTEX ENERGY in your calculation of the IDCs for November 15, 16 and 19.

TRANSITION JUNCTURE

During Transition the decreasing vibratory level of the current PLC and the increasing vibrations of the incoming PLC can sometimes create a measure of confusion. Each day of Transition contains its own unique blend of these two energies. The result of this is that it may become difficult to focus on any one area of interest.

The TRANSITION JUNCTURES (TJ) are designed to help solve this dilemma. These frequencies are steady and hold 100 percent throughout all three of the Transition Months—October, November and December. The way in which these months are influenced by the TJ number is by stabilization of the fluctuating PLC levels. It brings into focus the opportunities available during each month, taking into consideration the activity of the two PLCs and the inner control of the IMC. You can think of the TJ as a searchlight shining from the core of your Cycle activity, searching the dark sky for any opportunity that might be flying into your area of numerical structure.

There is only ONE Transition Juncture for all three months, and a new TJ is derived each year. Use the number and its energy level as a help in balancing the Transition Period and in discovering opportunities during that time.

Calculating the Transition Juncture

The TJs are especially helpful for those with Transition Birth-days. In delineating this Aspect, take into consideration the daily influence of both PLCs and of the IMC, which gives the way in which the PLCs are activated (see: Vol. I, Chapter 11, pp. 165–166).

Here are Peter's IMCs for the Transition Months:

PLC	MONTH	NUMBER			IMC NUMBER
7 +	October	10	= 1 =		8
7 +	November	*11		= 18 = 9	
7 +	December	12	= 3 =	10 = 1	

18 (Do not reduce)

ADD THE UNREDUCED DIGITS: 1+8=9 TJ 1987

Peter's TJ for the Transition Period of 1987 is NINE. Immediately we can see that during October, he should be attuned to his material welfare—finances, work or any other outlet for expression of the EIGHT. November then comes into exact alignment with his TJ of NINE. Through the efforts he made in October, Peter could then expand his horizons in November when the IMC of NINE conjuncts his TJ of NINE. This could bring in vital new opportunities for expansion. As Peter enters his third Transition Month, his IMC is the dominant ONE, which is still influenced 100 percent by his NINE TJ. Peter should discover a notable difference in his affairs and outlook as he comes to the end of 1987.

TRANSITION IMPEDIMENT

Understanding the vibrational activity of the Transition Period allows you to explore with confidence the dilemmas and opportunities for growth and action that occur during this important part of each year. The Transition Junctures highlight the best possible opportunities for us, pointing out the good, the bad, the possible and the impossible.

There is one more Transition Aspect whch enables us to securely lock in our intentions for that period—the TRANSITION IMPEDI-MENT (TI). You are by now familiar with how you can cope with the incoming and outgoing PLCs by using the TJ number to stabilize their fluctuating energies. However, in order to hold onto this valuable vibration throughout the Transition Period, you must take into account the influence of the TI.

This Aspect acts merely as a warning—it should not be thought of as a hostile or negative force. It's vital for you to understand just *how* the TI works:

1. If the power of the Transition Juncture is NOT being utilized, the Transition Impediment becomes activated. It's not uncommon for many people to operate during Transition by using the energies of the TI instead of the TJ.

2. Awareness of the TJ will activate ALL Aspects of the Chart, including the present status of the client's desires regarding ambition, vocation, goals, etc.

3. Allowing the TI to dominate will cause a concentration of force ONLY in the limited area of the TI vibrations. This is because it gives a feeling of force and direction, seeming to act as a motivating influence suggesting purpose and future progress.

4. Actually, what it does accomplish is in only a limited field of expression, causing an acceptance of what already exists, a feeling of willingness to "make do."

Calculating the Transition Impediments

Once again, we will use Peter's Chart:

PLC	MONTH	NUMBER			IMC NUMBER		
7	+ October	10	= 1	=	8		
7	+ November	*11		= 18	= 9		
7	+ December	12	= 3	= 10	= 1		

18 (Do not reduce)

SUBTRACT THE UNREDUCED DIGITS: 1−8=7 TI 1987

You see that the calculation is exactly the same as that for the TJ except that the digits of the total are SUBTRACTED instead of ADDED. This gives Peter a TI of SEVEN. If Peter found that for some reason he could not relax and take advantage of his TJ of NINE, the SEVEN TI would take over. It would be strongly supported by his decreasing PLC of SEVEN. This would suggest that the SEVEN was not decreasing as it should! He might have some difficulty in recognizing the daily degree increase of his incoming EIGHT PLC, as his area of concentration would be focused on the SEVEN. The TI, therefore, could turn Peter's thoughts and actions inward, thus preventing him from taking advantage of the wonderful start into his EIGHT PLC provided by his NINE TJ.

BALANCING TOOL

Let's suppose that Peter is experiencing difficulty in utilizing his TJ energies. You've seen how his outgoing PLC of SEVEN could support his TI of the same number. Another point to keep in mind is that ANY OTHER SEVEN in Peter's Natal Chart could *also* support the TI! Whenever you delineate the TJ and TI, *always* refer to the original Natal Chart to see whether these Transition Aspects are supported by existing Natal Aspects and if so, which ones. (For those of you interested in seeing which of Peter's Aspects match his SEVEN TI, consult the Analysis Summary of his Chart on page 191 of Vol. I.)

To help overcome the influence of the TI, he may refer to an Aspect called the BALANCING TOOL (BT), which is designed to lessen the effect of the TI and direct the focus toward the TJ.

Calculating the Balancing Tool

TRANSITION JUNCTURE	=	9
TRANSITION IMPEDIMENT	=	7
CURRENT PLC (1987)	=	7
TOTAL	23 =	5 BT 1987

The FIVE Balancing Tool would loosen any vibrational congestion in Peter's Transition Period, working with the NINE TJ to sever the holding power of the SEVEN TI.

Always calculate the BT when delineating Transition Procedures. It is a vital key which gives access to the incoming PLC energies and permits the remaining vibrations of the outgoing PLC to complete the full cycle needed to fulfill the goals of destiny.

CHAPTER 6

THE NATAL TRANSITION TABLE

The final Aspect to consider when dealing with the Transition Period is constructed whenever your client has a need to analyze a specific time period. This period can be either in the past or the future—it is a simple procedure to determine the PLC for any given year. Compiling a NATAL TRANSITION TABLE (NTT) will allow you latitude in your summary and analysis of the Transition Period.

The NTT is basically an instant PLC table, but it also includes the AGE of the client, which gives a clear picture of any period of time desired. Preparing the NTT eliminates the need for generalizing. The PLC changes are quite visible with young children; the parent normally sees them as changes in growth or personality. With Peter arriving under the Master influence of *11, he then demonstrated quite a contrast during his second PLC of THREE, which arrived at four months and seven days. His next PLC—FOUR—came in when he was sixteen months old and remained for another twelve months, up to the age of two years and four months. (We'll look at a complete NTT for Peter later on.)

When set up properly, the NTT shows clearly the age of the client and when he was under the influence of any particular PLC. It gives you more depth and accuracy when, for example, you know that a child had a PLC change at sixteen months instead of generalizing and assuming it to be during the child's second year.

SECTIONS OF THE NATAL TRANSITION TABLE

I have divided the NTT into FOUR sections, which cover the entire lifespan:

1. EARLY YEARS   = From birth to commencing school
2. SCHOOL YEARS   = Schooling through the 18th birthday
3. EARLY MATURITY = When PLC 9 is complete and Life Trinity Point #1 (LT1) is leaving (see: Vol. I, Chapter 11, pp. 136–137)
4. MATURITY   = Commences with a PLC of 1 and the entry of LT2 (see: Vol. I, Chapter 11, pp. 138–139)

The NTT can be started and finished for any period of time, according to the requirements of your client. If, for example, it's necessary to investigate a period of time beginning at nineteen years and ending at twenty-two years, you may prepare only that one section for analysis. However, I recommend that if time permits, a complete NTT be compiled. Then you will always have a full reference, ready to use at any time.

FINDING THE KEY

When preparing an NTT, you must use a KEY, which is the total of the BIRTH MONTH and DATE:

BIRTH MONTH = August = 8
BIRTHDAY   =   1   = <u>1</u>
                            9 = KEY

This KEY is then ADDED to the number of the CHRIST CYCLE for each year. This gives the PERSONAL LIFE CYCLE for each year.

KEY   =   9
1964 CC   =   <u>2</u>
              *11 = PLC *11 1964

NATAL TRANSITION TABLE FOR PETER PAUL CONNOLLY

Early Years

YEAR	CHRIST CYCLE		KEY		PLC	TIME PERIOD
1964 =	2	+ 9 =			*11	Birth–4 mos., 7 days
1965 =	3	+ 9 =	12	=	3	4 mos. 7 days–16 mos.
1966 =	*22	+ 9 =	31	=	4	16 mos.–2 yrs., 5 mos.
1967 =	5	+ 9 =	14	=	5	2 yrs., 5 mos.–3 yrs., 6 mos.
1968 =	6	+ 9 =	15	=	6	3 yrs. 6 mos.–4 yrs., 7 mos.
1969 =	7	+ 9 =	16	=	7	4 yrs., 7 mos.–5 yrs., 8 mos.
1970 =	8	+ 9 =	17	=	8	5 yrs., 8 mos.–6 yrs., 9 mos.

School Years

YEAR	CHRIST CYCLE		KEY		PLC	TIME PERIOD
1971 =	9	+ 9 =	18	=	9	6 yrs., 9 mos.–7 yrs., 10 mos.
1972 =	1	+ 9 =	10	=	1	7 yrs., 10 mos.–8 yrs., 11 mos.
1973 =	2	+ 9 =			*11	8 yrs., 11 mos.–10 yrs.
1974 =	3	+ 9 =	12	=	3	10 yrs.–11 yrs.
1975 =	*22	+ 9 =	31	=	4	11 yrs.–12 yrs.
1976 =	5	+ 9 =	14	=	5	12 yrs.–13 yrs.
1977 =	6	+ 9 =	15	=	6	13 yrs.–14 yrs.
1978 =	7	+ 9 =	16	=	7	14 yrs.–15 yrs.
1979 =	8	+ 9 =	17	=	8	15 yrs.–16 yrs.
1980 =	9	+ 9 =	18	=	9	16 yrs.–17 yrs.
1981 =	1	+ 9 =	10	=	1	17 yrs.–18 yrs.
1982 =	2	+ 9 =			*11	18 yrs.–19 yrs.

Early Maturity

YEAR	CHRIST CYCLE		KEY		PLC	TIME PERIOD
1983 =	3	+ 9 =	12 =		3	19 yrs.–20 yrs.
1984 =	*22	+ 9 =	31 =		4	20 yrs.–21 yrs.
1985 =	5	+ 9 =	14 =		5	21 yrs.–22 yrs.
1986 =	6	+ 9 =	15 =		6	22 yrs.–23 yrs.
1987 =	7	+ 9 =	16 =		7	23 yrs.–24 yrs.
1988 =	8	+ 9 =	17 =		8	24 yrs.–25 yrs.
1989 =	9	+ 9 =	18 =		9	25 yrs.–26 yrs. (Leaving LT1=8)
1990 =	1	+ 9 =	10 =		1	26 yrs.–27 yrs.(Entering LT2=1)

Maturity

YEAR	CHRIST CYCLE		KEY		PLC	TIME PERIOD
1991 =	2	+ 9 =			*11	27 yrs.–28 yrs.
1992 =	3	+ 9 =	12 =		3	28 yrs.–29 yrs.
1993 =	*22	+ 9 =	31 =		4	29 yrs.–30 yrs.
1994 =	5	+ 9 =	14 =		5	30 yrs.–31 yrs.
1995 =	6	+ 9 =	15 =		6	31 yrs.–32 yrs.

And so on. The Natal Transition Table can be continued on a year-by-year basis to any desired point.

CHAPTER 7

THE CONSULTANT'S
TRANSITION REFERENCE

We've covered a good deal of material in studying the Transition Period in the last three Chapters. This Chapter is devoted to a reference list to help you keep the pertinent elements in mind as you delineate a Transition Chart, preparing a Transition Grid, Natal Transition Wheel and Natal Transition Table. This reference is *not* intended for use as a substitute for diligent study and practice of the foregoing material, but merely as a help to you after you have become thoroughly familiar with Transition Aspects and Procedures.

1. Transition *begins* on OCTOBER 1 of each year.

2. Transition *ends* one minute after midnight on JANUARY 7 of each year.

3. The Personal Life Cycle (PLC) is activated at 100% efficiency on JANUARY 8 of each year and continues through SEPTEMBER 30 of each year.

4. During the month of SEPTEMBER, the PLC and the Individual Month Cycle (IMC) are *identical*.

5. OCTOBER is the Monitor Month (MM), giving a preview of the incoming PLC.

6. *Twice* each year the IMC is *identical* to the PLC for the *following year*; this occurs in JANUARY (Karmic Sun) and in OCTOBER (Monitor Month).

7. JANUARY is the month of the Karmic Sun, which has its exact effect on the *first day* of the Mystic Birth Cycle (MBC), JANUARY 1; its influence is sustained throughout the MBC, JANUARY 1–7.

8. Transition Birthdays (TB) are those which fall between OCTOBER 1 and JANUARY 7.

9. The Nature of Essence (NE) is found in the combination of the incoming and outgoing PLCs for Transition Birthdays.

10. The TransitionGrid (TG) is a graph that shows the percentages of incoming and outgoing PLCs for each of the 99 days of the Transition Period.

11. The Transition Mystic Cycle (TMC) is a period of 92 days covering the three *full months* of Transition, OCTOBER 1–DECEMBER 31.

12. The Mystic Birth Cycle (JANUARY 1–7) follows immediately after the TMC; on JANUARY 8, you experience 100% of your incoming PLC—this is your Esoteric New Year.

13. NOVEMBER 15 is the *mid-point* of the 92-day TMC; four days later, on NOVEMBER 19, the energies of the incoming and outgoing PLCs are *exactly equal* at 50% each.

14. The Esoteric Seed Day (ESD) occurs whenever the Original Plan (OP) is identical to the World Day Cycle (WDC).

15. The vibratory influence of the Individual Day Cycle (IDC) lasts at the same level for a total of *12 hours*.

16. The Daily Vibrational Level (DVL) can give you the "temperature" of the IDC, showing how the energies gradually increase and decrease over a 24-hour period.

17. The Exact Karmic Alignment (EKA) occurs only *once every nine years*, when the soul is in true alignment with the Original Karmic Intention; it occurs on the Physical Birthday (PB) that coincides with the OP.

18. The Vertex (VE) is the fusing of energies in all Aspects, Levels and Cycles, the fusing of *any two numbers* in the Natal Chart.

19. The Natal Transition Wheel (NTW) shows clearly and simply in graphic form how the various components of the Transition Period relate to one another.

20. The Esoteric Birthday (EB) occurs *exactly four months prior* to the actual Physical Birthday (PB).

21. The Transition Bridge Cycle (TBC) can be used to greatly enhance past-life regressions, with the calculation of a new TBC number each year; on the EB each year, past-life memories are at their strongest.

22. The Transition Juncture (TJ) occurs *once each year* for all three Transition months; its frequency holds steady at 100% throughout the three-month period and can be used to stabilize the fluctuating PLC energies.

23. The Transition Impediment (TI) is activated when the energy of the Transition Juncture is not utilized.

24. The Balancing Tool (BT) is used to activate the Transition Juncture and help mitigate the effects of the Transition Impediment.

25. The Consultant should compile a Natal Transition Table (NTT) whenever the client wishes to investigate a specific period, past, present or future.

CHAPTER 8

THE SPECTRUM BLOCK

The next tool for the advanced Gnothologist is not a simple one to master, but is an excellent one and well worth the effort it takes to become thoroughly familiar with it. It deals with the numerical values of the ORIGINAL FULL NAME AT BIRTH on three separate levels. It is called the SPECTRUM BLOCK (SPB).

When used properly, after you have developed fluency in interpreting each letter and the ability to connect the letters and understand their combined meanings, you'll find that the Spectrum Block provides a wonderful means of focusing on any specific area of life and seeing the vibratory forces at work there. With it you can cover the entire spectrum of numerical possibilities, past, present and future.

An ideal approach to this study is to work on your own Chart first. Begin by selecting a definite time period from your recent past for analysis. Select a time when you have a vivid recollection of what took place: events, emotions, relationships, etc. With this clearly in mind, you can then extract and examine this time period closely and see whether your skill at interpretation is accurate.

Most students initially want to project into the future, but I strongly advise working with the past first. Once you have come to rely upon your interpretive ability by working with a time period that can be verified, then you will feel confident in exploring the present or future or any aspect of the Spectrum Block.

The Spectrum Block contains the mystery of the soul's journey. This particular study requires both skill and concentration, but once you become accomplished in this area, you will indeed have earned your "wings" as a Consultant! You will need to take into account many other Aspects in a client's Chart when evaluating and summarizing the Spectrum Block. Intelligent cross-referencing will open the mystery of this intriguing study; failure to explore these current areas of activity thoroughly will not only limit your analysis but can cause it to be inaccurate.

SPECTRUM LEVELS

The Spectrum Block uses the FULL ORIGINAL BIRTH NAME only. Other names—through adoption, marriage, name changes, nicknames, etc.—are not applicable to this Aspect.

The Spectrum Block is comprised of FIVE Sub-Aspects called SPECTRUM LEVELS, arranged as you see on the Graph that follows. Each one has its own specific function within the Block.

Spectrum Level 1 (Line 1)

SPECTRUM LEVEL 1 (SL1) is the AGE LINE and begins with ZERO. At birth we immediately come under the influence of the FIRST letter of the FIRST NAME, but before the first birthday arrives, we must account for the period of the first twelve months, 0–12 (year 1). The age line can be extended to any desired age for the purpose of analysis.

Spectrum Level 2 (Line 2)

SPECTRUM LEVEL 2 (SL2) deals only with the FIRST NAME. Each letter of the first name is placed in the Graph *the number of times that equals the value of the letter*. Thus, in Peter's name, the first "P" (which is equivalent to SEVEN) is placed in the Graph *seven times*. The first "E" which follows equals FIVE, so it appears *five times*. The "T" appears *twice*, the second "E" *five times* and the final letter, "R," occupies *nine spaces*. Once you have completed the proper

Spectrum Block:

Note! Vacant lines can be used to enter pertinent information for reference when charting. Current year, PLC's, LT. Points, etc. See example:

Peter Paul Connolly:

Age	0	1	2	3	4	5	6	7	8	9	10	11	12	13	14	15	16	17	18	19	20	21	22	23	24	25	26	27	28	29	30	31	32	33	34
1st Name	P	P	P	P	P	P	P	P	P	E	E	E	E	E	E	E	E	E	R	R	R	R	R	R	R	R	R	P	P	P	P	P	P	P	P
2nd Name	P	P	P	P	P	P	A	U	U	L	L	L	P	P	P	P	P	P	A	U	U	L	L	L	P	P	P	P	P	P	A	U	U	L	L
Last Name	C	C	C	C	O	O	O	O	N	N	N	N	O	O	O	O	L	L	L	L	Y	Y	Y	Y	C	C	C	C	O	O	O	O	L	L	L
Matrix Total: →	8	8	8	2	2	2	2	3	5	7	7	1	1	9	9	9	9	1	1	6															

Age	35	36	37	38	39	40	41	42	43	44	45	46	47	48	49	50	51	52	53	54	55	56	57	58	59	60	61	62	63	64	65	66	67	68	69
1st Name	E	E	E	T	T	E	E	E	E	R	R	R	R	R	R	R	R	R	P	P	P	P	P	E	E	E	E	T	T						
2nd Name	A	U	U	L	L	P	P	P	P	A	U	U	L	L	L	P	P	P	P	P	P	A	U	U	L	L	L	P	P						
Last Name	O	O	O	N	N	N	N	O	O	O	O	L	L	L	Y	Y	Y	Y	C	C	C	C	O	O	O	O	L	L	N						
Matrix Total: →	3	5	5	1	1	8	8	9	9	9	7	6	6	6	3	3	3	8	8	8	3	5	5	5	7	11	1								

spacing of the first-name letters, simply continue to repeat this arrangement over and over for as long as you wish to sustain the Graph. (You'll note that Peter's Graph is extended to age 69.)

Spectrum Level 3 (Line 3)

SPECTRUM LEVEL 3 (SL3) deals only with the MIDDLE NAMES, and follows exactly the same procedure as Line 2. If there is more than one middle name, simply place them as they occur. For example Mary (Elizabeth Jean) Smith would have both middle names—Elizabeth and Jean—placed according to the numerical values of each letter, and then repeated as many times as necessary in the same order. If there is *no* middle name, leave Line 3 blank.

Spectrum Level 4 (Line 4)

SPECTRUM LEVEL 4 (SL4) deals only with the LAST NAME. The same procedure applies as in Lines 2 and 3.

Spectrum Level 5 (Line 5)

SPECTRUM LEVEL 5 is called the MATRIX (MX). It contains the TOTALS of all the numerical values of the lines directly above it and is actually composed of two separate lines—the *unreduced* totals and the *reduced* totals. Do *not* reduce Master Number totals of *11, *22 or *33. On Peter's Graph, for example, the first column adds up like this:

LINE 1: AGE	= O	
LINE 2: FIRST NAME	= P =	7
LINE 3: MIDDLE NAME	= P =	7
LINE 4: LAST NAME	= C =	3
LINE 5: MATRIX	=	17
TOTAL	=	8

(Note that the AGE FIGURE on Line 1 is NOT added into the Matrix total; only the numbers that correspond to the letters of the names are used.) Each column in the Spectrum Block is added up in the same manner.

The Matrix is the substance or general KEY to each computation. It is an overall guide which works with the O Level Aspects and combines all three PERSONAL LEVELS (to be explored in the following section). The Matrix is the combined total of these three levels, each of which corresponds to one of the Spectrum Levels (Lines 2, 3 and 4). When totalled to form the Matrix, the result reaches a SEED made up of these three levels. From this Seed you can determine the collective vibrations, thus obtaining a general sense of personality, expression and the incoming destiny during any period delineated.

Once again I must stress that exceptional care and sensitivity must be used in interpreting the Spectrum Block. The combined numerical forces create powerful tools for forecasting or for exploring the past. Consider the impact of any two numbers and understand fully what each number means. Pay special attention to the Vertex levels here: how the nature of each number being changed through its combining with another causes its interpretation to change according to the quantity and qualities of both numbers.

PERSONAL LEVELS

Within the Spectrum Block are THREE distinct PERSONAL LEVELS, each of which is associated ONLY with a specific part of the name:

1. PHYSICAL LEVEL   = FIRST NAME   (Spectrum Level 2)
2. EMOTIONAL LEVEL = MIDDLE NAMES   (Spectrum Level 3)
3. SPIRITUAL LEVEL   = LAST NAME   (Spectrum Level 4)

If there is no middle name, this level remains blank on the graph. However, this does not imply the lack of an Emotional Level—obviously everyone has one! It merely means that the Emotional Level is absorbed by the upper (Physical) and lower (Spiritual) levels. This will be obvious from the personality of the client.

In the Spectrum Block, the vibratory interpretations are ruled more by the LETTERS than the NUMBERS. For example, let's look at the letter "H"; we know that "H"=EIGHT. We also know that "Q" and "Z" also vibrate to this same number. When located in the Spectrum Block, each of these EIGHT-frequency letters will be interpreted according to the subtle differences it radiates.

Each of these three letters has three PERSONAL LEVELS of interpretation. Let's look at the PHYSICAL LEVEL of "H," "Q" and "Z," as if they were all contained in a client's FIRST NAME (yes, I know—it would have to be a pretty odd name!).

Physical Level: H=8

On the Physical Level you will experience severe highs and lows. The extremes of "H" are quite volatile. Unless you are well balanced, you may be caught up in radical and excessive behavior patterns. But the power of the EIGHT on the Physical Level can be beneficial if the energy it channels can be utilized properly. If not, there will be many periods of anxiety, indecision and uncertainty.

Physical Level: Q=8

As an adult you should benefit greatly from the "Q" of home, work, business and finances. This frequency also contains strong health vibrations, and those who have it usually feel exhilarated. Success is imminent and expectations are high.

Physical Level: Z=8

Under the influence of this vibration, you can see the results of previous efforts. The spade work has been completed, and now it's harvest time! If seeds have been sown there will be many rewards affecting the home, work, business and finances. Even later in life, projects can be initiated with confidence. Earlier in life, the EIGHT energies work differently with children.

THE VALUE OF THE SPECTRUM BLOCK

The above examples should show you how the EIGHT vibration has its own unique Physical Level interpretation for each letter. The same is true for the Emotional and Spiritual Levels as well. It is important that you understand the subtle but vital differences between each of the letters and Levels in order to utilize the true value of the Spectrum Block. Here we are touching upon Cycles within Cycles, and unless it is done with expertise, all the EIGHTS will appear identical.

The Matrix also has its own frequency, combining all three levels yet remaining isolated.

The heights and depths of the Spectrum Block are determined by the Original Level Aspects and the current Cycles, particularly the Life Opportunities (L.Opps), Life Obstacles (L.Obs) and Life Trinity Points (LT). Without these Aspects, the value of the Spectrum Block is wasted and its powers of analysis of past, present and future lost. You should always prepare yourself and your clients for the potential activity rooted in the Spectrum Block; don't allow all the other things happening in your life to deprive you of the time necessary to utilize this excellent Aspect to its fullest extent. Used correctly, it can motivate the client to approach his destiny in the most positive fashion; ignored, the Matrix energy will be wasted.

Until you have a thorough grasp of the various letter interpretations according to the three Personal Levels, it would be better to concentrate on the Matrix numbers. From them you can learn to get a general feel for the three vibratory forces as they merge with the current Cycles.

After you have mastered the letter energies, you will see how each of them has its own unique influence in the lives of your clients. You will be able to detect how they are being used and how your clients react to them.

CHILDREN AND THE SPECTRUM BLOCK

Children and young adults react quite differently from adults to the influences of the three Personal Levels. Early in life these Levels may or may not be activated, depending on circumstances surrounding the subject. Each Level has a different interpretation for infants, young children and teenagers. I am presently writing a book that will focus specifically on Gnothology for children. It will be a complete and comprehensive guide for parents, teachers and Consultants. It will cover in depth the impact of Aspects and Cycles on children and will include a section on how to analyze their Spectrum Block.

PERSONAL LEVELS OF THE ALPHABET

In this section, I will give you interpretations of each of the 26 letters of the alphabet on each of the three Personal Levels—Physical, Emotional and Spiritual. They should be studied with great care and you should take note of all the subtle shades of difference, as well as similarities.

Physical Level (First Name)

PHYSICAL LEVEL: A=1

At any age there could be unexpected changes: they can be the result of careful planning, or they can represent chaos and upheaval. These changes are likely to occur in the areas of home and business, finances, career and domestic life. They could encompass anything from winning the Lottery to declaring bankruptcy. You can anticipate this type of change by carefully analyzing the current Cycles and the rest of the Chart Aspects.

PHYSICAL LEVEL: J=1

During this "J" year there is a settled feeling; you are likely to be in touch with your true feelings and ideals. There is usually a slight increase in your affairs, accompanied by a sense of stability and reserve toward future planning. The application of common sense will provide confidence in matters of finance.

PHYSICAL LEVEL: S=1

This may be considered a time of frustration, but only in retrospect. It is a learning and developing time, and the end result should be satisfactory. The main body of the Chart will also reflect these indications. You must undergo the experiences that occur so that you can adjust your present life situation according to your path of destiny.

PHYSICAL LEVEL: B=2

This is a karmic period of learning how to deal with certain circumstances and relationships that appear. It is important not to give in to the tendency to withdraw from any opportunities which may also arise. Allowing insecurity to guide you at this point can lead to illness. Facing the challenges should result in a very positive experience—a chance to let go of fears pertaining to your own life path, to rid yourself of negative situations and relationships that are stifling your personal progress and happiness. It will give you the opportunity to start over with new and brighter plans.

PHYSICAL LEVEL: K=2

The "K" has a multiple effect! Its power can be felt throughout the Chart. Used correctly, it can be exciting and exhilarating. But its intense vibrations may exclude important areas of concentration, and lack of depth and focus can cause constant dilemmas. So beware of living for the moment and not taking time to analyze situations thoroughly. Don't be overly concerned with unimportant daily events; operating solely through the emotions and not thinking ahead can have devastating consequences and cause hurt and misunderstandings in relationships.

PHYSICAL LEVEL: T=2

The intensity of the "T" vibration is not fully expressed or experienced until the adult years. Upon reaching maturity, you are presented with expansion by the "T"—a need to investigate, experiment and learn. The karmic forces expand and your mind is filled with thoughts of new places and new kinds of work. This is the opportune time to consider new ideas and let go of exising fears and self-imposed restrictions.

PHYSICAL LEVEL: C = 3

Up to about the age of 13 the "C" has its own identity on the Physical Level. From that age on you are in an expressive period, with a constant desire for personal creativity and outward personal expression. This is a unique period, a delicate time capsule in which it is possible to touch upon the heights of past-life endeavors. This may result in a surge of personal creativity which has hitherto been submerged.

PHYSICAL LEVEL: L = 3

The second year is the middle pillar of this three-year period, the year when the Physical "L" releases its energy with a 100-percent impact! Opportunity is created—an urge to move, travel or change in some manner to accomodate the opportunity, whatever it may be. Good health is associated with the "L" at this level, and the vibratory force is one of energy and excitement. It would be most unfortunate to resist this energy. Check the remainder of your Chart to see how the energy can be used for your best advantage.

PHYSICAL LEVEL: U = 3

Here you have the exact opposite to the vibration of the sister letter "L" above! This is a time to avoid extremes and change, to consider present situations carefully and postpone important decisions, especially during the second year of this three-year period. Excess behavior patterns must be moderated to avoid loss. Challenge is the lesson here, and you must confront it. Prepare to build up your inner strength, conserve your energy and avoid the temptation to make drastic moves. Look to the future—this is not the time to experiment.

PHYSICAL LEVEL: D = 4

Foundations and plans need to be solidified at this time by contacts which may involve movement and travel. It is a time of planning and preparation, bringing a need to explore, negotiate and perhaps bargain. Feelings may be divided, and you may feel insecure as the need for making the decision becomes vital to the family, lifestyle, business and home. You will feel the pull of two directional forces, but it is your karma to make this decision at this time. Avoiding it will result in regret and insecurity later.

PHYSICAL LEVEL: M=4

This Physical "M" Level is your anchor! Hold fast to what you have—it's unwise to venture into unknown areas of life experience at this time. This could necessitate a residential move to secure your roots. Expenses must be considered and your home base must feel secure. This is not the time to become involved in financial or other changes that are not secure. The focus now is on your health—don't become involved in situations that can affect your physical stability through tension, stress or worry.

PHYSICAL LEVEL: V=4

Karmic friendships and relationships can be renewed under this "V" influence. The fourth year of this sequence can be quite invigorating! The first three years can introduce many new situations in which unusual circumstances can bring unexpected opportunities. Health and vitality appear to increase. Love, friendship and group karma can come together at this time. Satisfaction can be gained through sincere efforts as long as consideration is displayed for all concerned.

PHYSICAL LEVEL: E=5

Look for progressive change during this five-year period. Highs and lows are governed by the Physical "E." Personality and outlook undergo changes resulting in new endeavors that dominate finance and business affairs. Children react to this vibration at an early age; rapid development occurs and the need to deal with positive and negative situations accelerates a mature attitude. Many varied paths offer many unusual opportunities at this time. The Chart should reveal the capacity to recognize and accept them.

PHYSICAL LEVEL: N=5

This vibration acts as a thermometer in regard to future activities, revealing certain relationship patterns that will be affected by the incoming "N." It may appear that the first two years of this period have little or no direction, but when the third year begins it brings about the conclusive energies that were initiated during the first year. These unforced changes are karmic in nature and act in a protective manner. The third year will begin to bring in the harvest due.

PHYSICAL LEVEL: W=5

Balance and equilibrium are affected by this Level; the least provocation can upset the delicate balance of life's progress. Karma is testing you throughout this whole Spectrum period. Control and moderation are your keys to stabilization. In dealing with the "W" it's important to know that the *Emotional Level* dominates throughout this period. Many obstacles will appear in your life path in order to provide the challenge demanded by karma, and you must look for your strength in the current Cycles and Aspects, especially the Life Opportunities (L.Opps).

PHYSICAL LEVEL: F=6

Children will be aware of responsibility and parental attitudes. As an adult you will be involved in various levels of responsibility—others will lean on you and become dependent, which may cause you to rebel against the situation. This would not be wise, for the acceptance of responsibility will bring you meaningful growth throughout the six years of this influence. Resistance can only cause imbalance, while meeting the challenge means passing the test and completing any karmic obligations involved.

PHYSICAL LEVEL: O=6

This is a fortunate vibration for a child; in maturity it demands the input of tranquility. Balance must be retained at all costs. Leadership is usually thrust upon you, and a gradual increase in responsibility begins to bring in its rewards during the fourth Transition Period of this Spectrum Level. The fruits of this period may remain just out of reach if you become impatient and lose your sense of tranquility and balance. Patience and self-control will bring rewards.

PHYSICAL LEVEL: X=6

The sensitivity of the Physical "X" is difficult for the child, but from the sixteenth year of Transition the effect of this vibratory Level is to allow him to connect with his past-life talents. From this can grow achievement in many areas in life and the possibility of establishing a wide reputation. You should avoid the tendency to be secretive and reclusive at this time, as great success is associated with the Physical "X" energies, beginning after the third Transition Period of this six-year sequence. The challenge here is to be willing to share your talents and be recognized for them.

PHYSICAL LEVEL: G=7

This Level is divided into three nine-year segments of activity, covering years 1 through 27. Each segment presents emotional and educational challenges. As they occur, there is a tendency to withdraw and internalize them and there is a great feeling of being misunderstood, which causes the child to become secretive. However, after the Transition Period of his 27th year, the Level stabilizes. With the arrival of the incoming PLC, which repeats his first PLC, his nature unfolds and leadership qualities surface. He will develop a deep desire to change social and/or economic situations through humanitarian efforts in writing, teaching, politics, etc.

PHYSICAL LEVEL: P=7

The Physical "P" child can be quick-minded and impressionable. It's important that his parents and teachers have a good relationship with him, otherwise the child will withdraw totally. Hidden knowledge is accompanied by frustration as the child grows and develops. The adult also experiences emotional highs and lows. He is reliable yet unpredictable, sensitive and hungry to reach a satisfactory level of achievement. Not content with the average, he always wants to express his best and has an inner yearning to succeed. Close rela-tionships are important. Past wisdom will surface as he seeks the meaning of life.

Physical Level: Y = 7

This vibration is unconcerned with the material aspects of life. Emotions are tied in closely with the spiritual aspect. With this "Y" energy, you can become almost too content with your situation, as it tends to attract all you need with little effort. This Spectrum Level is not entirely Physical, therefore there is a tendency to feel discon-nected or unconcerned about life. As this seven-year period decreases, the balance begins to adjust. You are likely to feel this adjustment through your physical body, as there will be minor concerns about health to deal with. Clumsiness can cause minor accidents, so be care-ful! You will respond immediately to the full vibratory rate of the in-coming Level.

Physical Level: H = 8

On this Level you will experience severe highs and lows. The ex-tremes of "H" are quite volatile. Unless you are well balanced, you may be caught up in radical and excessive behavior patterns. But the power of the EIGHT on the Physical Level can be beneficial if the energy it channels can be utilized properly. If not, there will be many periods of anxiety, indecision and uncertainty. This Level is especially difficult for children, since they tend to see life as either black or white. Thus, it is hard for them to be moderate.

Physical Level: Q = 8

The vibratory impact of the Physical "Q" arrives during the PLC of EIGHT, from the age of 22 on. Before that time it lies dormant in the child and teenager. Only under extreme circumstances would it be seen in a child. Then it would manifest as a genius for mathematics. As an adult, you should benefit greatly from the "Q" vibration of EIGHT: life can expand in all directions and restriction is unheard of. Income will improve greatly as your talents and abilities are put to use. Self-expression is vital, for success is imminent and expectations are high. If restriction is felt in any area, you should move to a new location to fulfill your destiny. Strong health vibrations also accompany this Level.

PHYSICAL LEVEL: Z = 8

The child will be competitive under this vibration, and his ego can be very fragile until he reaches maturity. The importance of achieving and winning may be uppermost in his mind. Upon reaching maturity, he will see his world open up as all kinds of opportunities are presented to him. As an adult, you can now see the end results of previous efforts. Your mind will operate better on large-scale projects. This personality is ideal for leadership, but the energy should be used wisely. You should allow others to contribute—don't try to do it all yourself.

PHYSICAL LEVEL: I = 9

The extremely sensitive Physical "I" can present early problems. The child is extremely aware of his surroundings and associates himself with the vibratory forces of others. His health may be affected if this causes undue strain. He is especially vulnerable if exposed to unbalanced situations. As an adult you are also open to the vibrations of others, and this can create tension and a desire to be alone. It's difficult for you to relax fully, as you seem to have a continuous stream of energy. If tensions become too great, you may withdraw entirely. It's important to try to maintain your balance, as your health may be affected. Midway into this nine-year period you should avoid speculation, since this could result in loss.

PHYSICAL LEVEL: R = 9

The Physical "R" is a steady vibration that influences the entire span of life. Care should be taken regarding health and balance. The child is very sensitive and loving and so is the adult, but neither can prosper unless they are exposed to loving and supportive relationships. Unless they have a balanced background and support they may become introverted and withdrawn. They thrive on love and have a tremendous potential to bring great light into the world. They also thrive on balance, and a sensitive, loving person can bring out all their natural talents.

Emotional Level (Middle Name)

EMOTIONAL LEVEL: A = 1

An undercurrent of activity blending with the existing Spectrum Levels will create multiple changes which will concern home, business and health. The focus should be on the current Cycles and Aspects. It should then be directed toward the Matrix. Past-life incidents can affect the present balance, so it is advisable to understand why the changes are occurring. Invest your strength and determination in situations that hold value in this life. The child will feel this vibration as temporary periods of insecurity.

EMOTIONAL LEVEL: J = 1

The Emotional "J" produces a great impact on the child, giving him much responsibility. It can be an exceptionally trying period of experience for him. After age 20 the nature of the vibration is centered in a fixed personality aspect, which can cause you to become very single-minded and opposed to any advice or opinions from others. As the year enters the Transition Period, you will become more defensive, but as the energy decreases you will begin to look toward new horizons.

EMOTIONAL LEVEL: S = 1

A strong karmic aspect comes with the Emotional "S," highlighting relationships. Deep feelings are stirred up, and you will learn the importance of knowing how to deal with others. Spiritual growth is emphasized, for the child has known his parents before! There is also the need to discard the unwanted and learn how to go on toward new opportunities. Emotions will be tested and the need to be in control will increase. Many lessons are learned during this karmic "S" year.

EMOTIONAL LEVEL: B=2

This is not a comfortable vibration for the young child. Emotions are quickly aroused and much understanding is needed from parents and teachers. As the child enters his teen years the vibratory rate alters and the energy becomes more positive. The karmic tendency is toward understanding and tolerance. Until the age of 36, and especially between the Transition of the 16th year through the Transition of the 25th year, relationships will be examined and tested. Karmic dues will be paid. Balance and proportion will prevail in all relationships. The clearing of past karma will ultimately bring into view the right partner for this life.

EMOTIONAL LEVEL: K=2

This is time for self-review. During this two-year Level many obstacles appear. Karmic adjustment is in progress. Disinterest and self-doubt present situations in which you are forced to make decisions. Usually you emerge from this period with new and exciting ideas, like the butterfly breaking out of its chrysalis. New vision and courage fortify these new beginnings with hope and joy. The child can appear difficult during this period, but he is usually content to be on his own and enjoys his secretive life of make-believe.

EMOTIONAL LEVEL: T=2

This is the center of the Emotional "T." At the age of 13 the child rapidly becomes aware of his emotional needs. From the age of 15 on he experiences an increased interest in love and marriage which grows as the teenage years develop. A searching for completion in a karmic relationship can lead to intriguing situations later in life. A serious attitude prevails and a need to be appreciated is shown in all relationships. Once you have found the right partner you will be loyal, reliable and loving to your family. You'll experience a feeling of incompleteness until this karmic relationship once again connects. But during the search you may experience unhappiness if you choose the wrong partner.

EMOTIONAL LEVEL: C=3

This is a freedom-loving three-year cycle for all ages. Serious relationships should not be encouraged, for it's likely they won't last. You need to express yourself in many ways, for your talents will surface and you can be exceptionally charming during these years. Children thrive with the right kind of guidance from their parents. The soul enjoys the vibratory aspect of personal freedom, a need to travel and explore. Travel is ideal for the adult, and variety of expression should be encouraged in the child.

EMOTIONAL LEVEL: L=3

The Emotional "L" is a fortunate Level for both child and adult. Relationships established during this period are usually long-lasting and beneficial. Soul mates are discovered and marriage is successful on this Level. During their early teen years, young people often experience frustration if they have to wait before they can be together. All in all, this is a happy period of discovery. The vibratory rate also induces creative talents. I consider this Level to be a pleasant karmic gift to be understood and enjoyed. Children born on this Level carry the joy associated with it throughout life.

EMOTIONAL LEVEL: U=3

Here we have the opposite vibratory energy! The child needs encouragement and a constant show of love. The adult has to deal with strong feelings of depression. You should analyze the Chart in detail and highlight the positive Aspects prevailing during these three years to offset the negativity associated with the Emotional "U." Look to the positive aspect of the PLCs and focus on the powerful structure of your O-Level Chart. By taking this approach, you'll see the "U" gradually diminish in its effect. This is because it's like a fire: it needs continual fanning to blaze away, but pour on water and it will subside.

EMOTIONAL LEVEL: D=4

The child does not feel the impact of the Emotional "D" during his early years. After the Transition Period of the 14th year, the vibratory power begins to make itself felt. During this period you may feel a sense of fear and/or danger under certain conditions. With the focus on yourself, you may become very self-critical, develop a nervous disposition and concentrate too much on your health. Search your Chart for positive outgoing Cycles and Aspects. This should eliminate the insecurity felt on this Level.

EMOTIONAL LEVEL: M = 4

Here the personality experiences internal conflict! On the surface everything appears fine and rosy, but on the inside you may experience doubt and insecurity. You are willing to go to any length to secure your life partner. Your ways will be secretive if you consider it necessary. You can say one thing but inside mean another. This inner contradiction can upset your security; you'll often try to ignore this situation by becoming excessive in some habit pattern. The child is usually outgoing and happy but suffers from inner confusion. It's always wise to explain the situation to a child on this Level or he will hold his feelings inside and never share them.

EMOTIONAL LEVEL: V = 4

This is an extremely beneficial Spectrum Level for both child and adult. During this four-year period there is contentment and happiness. Karma is being repaid on a wonderful level of life experience. Children are returning to old karmic ties and relationships and adults are just discovering them. From the age of 21 on there is a rapid increase in energy relating to career, vocation and/or talents. If worked upon this will bring much pleasure to the life path. The road of destiny appears to be wide and open. Obstacles can only generate if allowed to do so. It's easy for the Emotional "V" to fall into the rhythm of the positive aspect of the four PLCs. This should be encouraged, for this soul can find its purpose on this Level.

EMOTIONAL LEVEL: E = 5

As an adult you will experience a shifting or movement in your affairs. During this process there may be a sense of regret or disappointment. This will be followed after a short period of contemplation by long, binding relationships and a new sense of purpose. The child reacts to this vibratory power differently, by emotional demonstrations. He may demonstrate behavior and become outwardly demanding. After the third Transition of this five-year period, the child will adjust and settle down as the vibratory energy subsides.

EMOTIONAL LEVEL: N = 5

This can be a trying period! The difficulties are related to the emotions in a very direct manner. Many new relationships will come into being, each with its own karmic influence. The heart desires to find its true mate; this can create havoc as you endeavor to determine what love really is! Challenge and lack of stability can propel you into areas of insecurity. With children, firm roots are required: parents must be willing to demonstrate their love. The child is beset with fears and may retire into himself and nurse his feelings in silence.

EMOTIONAL LEVEL: W = 5

Emotional expansion comes with the "W." The child finds it difficult to cope with this vibratory influence. Being always willing to venture and experiment can result in a bruised ego. Parents should monitor this and offer guidance, so that the child does not suffer from continual disappointment which he may see as continual denial. This high vibratory frequency is ideal if you have specific goals. Without goals you'll feel frustrated as you strive toward your desired ambitions. You may have a tendency to overdo, gamble and experiment.

EMOTIONAL LEVEL: F = 6

As the child grows and develops he will realize early in life the meaning of responsibility. He may appear to be quite mature in his outlook and this should be encouraged. His karmic path should be calm and pleasant during his early days. In the FIRST sixth year AFTER the age of 12 he will be drawn to karmic situations in which he must demonstrate his sense of responsibility. This will involve him and all those dear to him. This strong karmic power will eventually bring him to his pinnacle of success as long as he recognizes *all* those who cross his life path.

Emotional Level: O=6

A great sense of inner security rests within the Emotional "O." The child will undergo adjustment during the first two years, thriving on the inner knowledge and balance that provide a good level of contentment and progress. After the age of 14 a natural flow of energies will bring about new and beneficial situations, and a sense of harmony should prevail. The second half of this six-year period can result in long-lasting relationships such as marriage, births, business partners, etc.

Emotional Level: X=6

The high frequency of this vibratory sequence releases unwanted and superfluous circumstances, with results that can be either positive or negative, depending upon the balance of the child or adult. Its purpose is to release all that prevents the desired level of harmony on your life path. Consequently, if this is not recognized trauma can result from resistance. The Emotional "X" makes way for the original intent of the soul to complete its destiny. There are really no highs or lows here when you consider that the ultimate purpose is to create success and achievement.

Emotional Level: G=7

This level could be considered the "Task Master." Its influence appears to force you to look, correct and readjust. It contains power which will spread into other Spectrum Levels if discipline is not maintained. "Purpose" is the keyword: during this seven-year period past talents and uncompleted efforts will rise to the consciousness. This can be difficult for the child and he may become shy, restrained, secretive and moody. But with support from his parents he may express unusual and surprising abilities. The Emotional "G" is a time for the inner purpose and talents to mature and a time to prepare for the future.

EMOTIONAL LEVEL: P = 7

At any age the Emotional "P" retains its air of mystery. Parents and teachers will see great potential and rapid development *if* the child is so inclined! He is old beyond his years; this can cause misunderstandings if not recognized. He is forever watching and establishing goals, yet he can be quiet, secretive and exceptionally sensitive. The adult years bring a focus which can be thought of as restraint. Personal relationships are important and necessary for you to build your foundations in life. Once your purpose becomes obvious, confusion will disappear and unlimited energies will vitalize your goals.

EMOTIONAL LEVEL: Y = 7

The Emotional "Y" finds its roots on this Level. It can be difficult to completely understand the influence of this vibration. At any age you will see the seeker and the results of his experiments! Education, study, home, relationships are all open to re-evaluation! The child shows unusual interests and will pursue his curiosity to the limits. The young adult will also pursue his curiosity and become involved in all kinds of experiences and experiments. Intense interests will develop during the mature years, resulting either in achievement or severe disappointment. Control is the answer: if this energy is harnessed and put to good use, you will have an exciting life of fulfilled dreams and goals.

EMOTIONAL LEVEL: H = 8

This Level brings struggle: struggle to achieve, struggle to be recognized, struggle to be loved. Power is associated with the Emotional "H"—the power of the lion who stalks behind the playful kitten. Never underestimate the "H." As long as you provide substantial support, he will be lovable and faithful. But room must be allowed for his ego. Unless he feels outward support he feels great inner conflict. His insecurity will make him expressive and dominant. He needs to succeed in love and career. If he feels threatened you'll see the pussycat become the King of the Jungle.

EMOTIONAL LEVEL: Q=8

This is a karmic period of adjustment and recognition of life's purpose. The child is quite open and vulnerable to outside influences, easily hurt and with a tendency to withdraw. The adult appears to have the unusual skill of going in the wrong direction! Many lessons are learned during this life period. Relationships can take a back seat as the energy compels you to totally immerse yourself in the life situation before you. As the Emotional "Q" propels you through life's ups and downs, your bruises show in your constant failures. Once you recognize the need for discipline, you'll be on your way to success as this period ends.

EMOTIONAL LEVEL: Z=8

This extrovert vibration is obvious at any age. After the 16th year Transition, the young adult will begin to show signs of ability. He will exercise his mental and physical energies toward the success he feels is important. After the age of 18, when the Emotional "Z" is activated, unusual opportunities, talents and experiences will occur. The power will focus in areas of achievement, leaving little time for close relationships. The child will be boisterous and outgoing and his parents will need to encourage his feelings of confidence, otherwise he will try to impose his needs by boasting, "proving" himself and domineering whenever he can. At any age this Level can cause a driving force with an apparent unconcern for the feelings of others. This is because he is focused into his own Emotional Level, being self-protective and outgoing.

EMOTIONAL LEVEL: I=9

Essential changes arrive during this period. The first four years present circumstances that speak of future change. They should not be overlooked or ignored. The fifth year is the turning point and will direct you to the needed action. If you show resistance, you could experience uncertainty, opposition and perhaps turmoil during the last four years of this nine-year cycle. Children will be exposed to meaningful early changes concerning home, family and school. It's essential that they be shown love and support, otherwise they will become insecure and nervous. Adults will have a tendency to hold on to situations that are not right for them, so "release" is the keyword here.

EMOTIONAL LEVEL: R=9

You should look first to the letter *preceding* and *following* the Emotional "R." Both of these letters carry the essential formula for middle NINE years. Taken only by itself this vibration has no support and can be considered a release mechanism. Planning with the preceding and following letters allows a more acceptable release. Karma plays an important part during these years: it compels you to adhere to your karmic path. Losses can be incurred, and relationships that are not meant to be will be severed. Emotions rule and can easily govern the head. Avoid unnecessary emotional situations whenever possible, as both adults and children will be exposed to unstable circumstances.

Spiritual Level (Last Name)

SPIRITUAL LEVEL: A=1

All ages find this Level beneficial. Progress and advancement are experienced during this important year. New ideas and inspiration emerge from the higher consciousness. As a result of this high vibrational level of energy, the following year should bring vast improvements in your life. Children feel uplifted and restrictions in learning patterns are eliminated. This surge of spiritual energy releases negativity that has blocked progress to date. Failure to recognize this vital force can cause false visions: the ego will expand beyond the normal level of acceptance, both in children and adults.

SPIRITUAL LEVEL: J=1

The Spiritual "J" does not have the same impact as "J" on other Levels. During this one-year period individuality is in focus and impatience is quick to surface. In the haste to complete projects and plans there may be a lack of depth. It's easy to make errors under this influence. In children you may see a lack of concentration in important areas, which will be reflected in school work. Adults may ignore current responsibilities in their efforts to create new ones! The high frequency of this vibration pushes thoughts outward and into the future. The lesson here is to deal with *now* and *then* look ahead.

SPIRITUAL LEVEL: S=1

This is a good year for introspection: self and purpose are inwardly analyzed. Often during this year new insights and goals are developed. Children see hints of their future. Steps should be taken to solidify your present status. It's an excellent time to take inventory. True desires surface, and negative blocks are seen objectively and can be eliminated. All age levels are extra sensitive now and are easily offended. As strength and inner wisdom solidify, this tendency disappears and the energy increases and is molded according to the future. New confidence and control must overcome overly sensitive feelings. This is the challenge of the Spiritual "S."

SPIRITUAL LEVEL: B=2

On the Spiritual Level the "B" does not hold much influence. Concentration should be on Physical and Emotional aspects. Relationships are highlighted, and there is a tendency to allow responsibility to shift within them, to allow others to take over and to rely on their guidance and opinions, even to your disadvantage. The child will seem less aggressive and also show a dependency on others. These things should be watched and avoided. The next incoming letter should point the way and help you make decisions regarding your self and your future.

SPIRITUAL LEVEL: K=2

This is a karmic level which will bring beneficial conclusions. During this two-year period there should be an increase in success. This Level can highlight sudden and unexpected turns on the life path, and these unusual and beneficial opportunities should be activated to bring about the karmic intent. The child will demonstrate an unusual capacity for learning. The adult will receive new inspirational thoughts. A clear path is shown and you should be encouraged to take that direction to the prosperity and success you desire. Activities will vary and new people will become involved in your life path.

SPIRITUAL LEVEL: T = 2

These two years are a time for reflection. You should take the time to look at your past and see how it now relates to your present. During the Spiritual "T" Level it is beneficial to contemplate past mistakes and make sure they are not repeated. Under the age of 14 the child will find it difficult to understand this energy. Parents may consider encouraging new friendships or changing schools. This period of inner growth can result in wisdom for the future. It is an excellent learning period. Much can be achieved in two years—they should not be allowed to drift by. Goals established now can come into fruition. Patience and concentrated efforts will be rewarded.

SPIRITUAL LEVEL: C = 3

Here is a remarkable three-year period that represents joy and future happiness. "Clarity" is the keyword! Many will receive exceptional future vision. Natural talents and abilities come into focus and method and procedure become comparatively easy. Tension and pressures are lifted, allowing you space to explore every possibility around you. Parents and teachers should be attuned to the child, for they may recognize hidden talents that the child may take for granted. All levels of personal expression should bring about successful results. From the 14th Transition Period these talents should surface and become obvious. You should encourage every outlet. To fully enjoy and benefit from the Spiritual "C" Level you must go with the tide and all that is meant to be will surface naturally.

SPIRITUAL LEVEL: L = 3

This Level should be highlighted on all Charts. It's always a fortunate period regardless of age. The adult should be open for extraordinary events resulting in success beyond his comprehension. It is advisable to look back and reconsider plans that were not activated, for this may be the right time for them to materialize. Young children are adaptable and open to learning processes. They can be wise beyond their years. The teenager can discover unusual opportunities now. The young adult can establish his future plans, and the mature adult can reap a harvest from his past experience.

SPIRITUAL LEVEL: U=3

This is a testing period, a time to explore your own dominion. Don't look to others for the guidance you need; become involved in your own spirituality. Karmic influences will show you new directions. Let go of the past and don't concern yourself with past losses. Dwelling upon the past can only negate future possibilities. Feeling sorry for yourself will put distance in your relationships. Although you may try to criticize those you feel responsible for your present dilemmas, no one will want to take the blame. This is not the right way to go. Children react to this vibratory force through insecure behavior. Parents should encourage them in all their ventures, thus dispelling their fear and insecurity.

SPIRITUAL LEVEL: D=4

The solid vibrational FOUR is challenged during this four-year period. Every effort should be made to re-establish your roots. Firm and reliable vibratory forces are available if you are determined to make a conscious effort. In the scattered influence of the Spiritual "D" there may be a false sense of pleasure, but this will quickly disappear and you will be brought to the center of your balance for further testing. The Spiritual strength of this Level can be found in foundations and set plans. Without these tools the vibratory force will continue to scatter every effort. Children need special protection and guidance during the formative years. They must learn to conserve, study and plan for the future.

SPIRITUAL LEVEL: M=4

Through past-life experiences you are now at the point in this life where you may feel at a loss. Everything appears to be under pressure. But this is a karmic period of four years during which you will be able to turn your whole life around! Only through your own efforts can this manifest, so you must use the strength gained from this Level. Depending on others will delay your goals. Through the 13th year of Transition children must be protected from self-defeat, for they will be inclined to accept life as it is. This is not the answer. After the 14th year they should be ready to accept responsibility, which will come in many forms. As an adult you must discover your own potential during these four years of spiritual growth.

Spiritual Level: V = 4

A highly spiritual vibratory energy remains for the full period of four years. The mind is cleared of doubt and insecurity; everything seems possible and worth working toward. The child is able to hold onto long-term goals. Past talents may be repeated in this life: this could be called a payment period! In some past-life endeavor you didn't receive full recognition for your efforts, so in this life you will be given a further opportunity to benefit from those efforts. The Spiritual "V" will clear the way for the future. Look at these four years as a grounding and learning period with a great harvest to come.

Spiritual Level: E = 5

Personal joy should be your quest now. The Spiritual Level of the FIVE can bring this joy, which can remain throughout life. Unfortunately, you may become compulsive and erratic in your behavior, causing opportunities to collapse. This vibratory force can isolate the "E" in certain areas of experience that others may find unacceptable. The spiritual lesson contained on this Level is to use the elasticity of the FIVE for personal growth. Develop a strong outlook, be versatile but not irresponsible. Plan methodically and don't rely on others. The challenge of the Spiritual "E" can bring about unexpected circumstances that will provide for the multifaceted aspect of FIVE. Children will be outgoing and versatile. Adults should use this energy to expand their goals.

Spiritual Level: N=5

The directive forces of this Level come in the form of conscience! You'll be forever trying to judge past, present and future decisions. The karmic lesson here is knowing how to forgive yourself. Feeling guilty and holding back for fear of what might happen can paralyze all attempts at success in any area. Through the 12th Transition the child may be shy and timid. Parents should watch for this influence, as it will affect his progress in personality and education. Fear is also felt in the teenager and adult. To offset this fear the teenager may become overly confident and aggressive. As an adult you may convince yourself that everything you want to do is far too risky! But it's important to face these fears, for in doing so you can release them.

Spiritual Level: W=5

During the five years of the Spiritual "W" other Levels are emphasized. The Spiritual Level appears dormant as the remaining Levels combine and govern. You may feel a lapse in faith, or you may begin searching for the truth. This impulse to discover purpose and God can become a driving force. The many experiences you'll encounter will bring you face to face with your own reality. Children readily take for granted the spiritual values of parents, teachers, etc., so it's important that teenagers not be exposed to fanatics, strange cults and exotic religions. Because of an unspoken need they are apt to become devout followers of any strongly organized group. *Gnothi seauton* (Know thyself) is the karma to be met.

Spiritual Level: F=6

"Tranquility" is the keyword for the Spiritual "F." A natural spiritual growth develops: you are content with your inner balance and the air of tranquility attracts favorable vibratory forces. Faith can be very strong on this Level. Tapping into the higher levels of consciousness, you'll take everything in your stride. It's not uncommon to meet souls you have known in a previous lifetime. Children up to the age of 13 are open, generous and kind. They seem content, regardless of home and background conditions. Unfortunately, they may be taken advantage of because they are extremely giving. This same pattern of the Spiritual "F" continues through any age Level.

SPIRITUAL LEVEL: O=6

A deep-seated desire to understand the laws of God and man are always uppermost on this "O" Level. Children will ask many questions about relationships, home and God. These questions should be answered, for they are an essential part of the child's growth. After the age of 13 you may see an accelerated growth in his spirituality. Life will present challenges and the "O" will volunteer his skills. The need to solve the world's problems is the level of spirituality that is the most satisfactory. Men and women both have the need to feel in harmony with all that is happening around them. For six years this vibratory force penetrates the mind. Bridges will be crossed to achieve karmic goals. Be content, all is well.

SPIRITUAL LEVEL: X=6

This is a developing and learning period of six full years. Expect a high degree of input relating to ability and comprehension. Knowledge from past lives seeps into the consciousness, expanding all levels of possibility. Both child and adult derive a deeper understanding of all things. This must not be thought of as negative or timidity, for the Spiritual "X" is exceptionally active and you will receive a remarkable ability to learn and digest. This unique process sharpens all the senses and the intuitive level becomes alert and receptive. Children under this influence are not necessarily outgoing and can be misjudged or thought of as quiet and retiring. Both child and adult will emerge from this Level feeling satisfied, educated and skilled.

SPIRITUAL LEVEL: G=7

The Spiritual "G" directs itself mostly to the Emotional Level. The Spiritual lesson must be experienced and controlled from that particular Level. As a result of this process we find that the Spiritual Level is enhanced by the ability to control the "G" on the Emotional

Level. After this seven-year period you will find that the following letter in the name on the Spiritual Level will be the key to your personal pattern of success. Through the 11th year of Transition the child may seem quiet and even difficult, but much is going on within him: he is assimilating the Spiritual activity through his Emotional Level. This is not easy. As an adult you may also appear withdrawn and often uncooperative. Releasing your thoughts and feelings will make way for incoming wisdom.

SPIRITUAL LEVEL: $P=7$

Children on this Spectrum Level often give the wrong impression. They find much comfort within themselves. An unusual sense of independence enables them to live in their own world and they find it difficult to communicate their knowledge. Consequently, a parent or teacher may conclude that the child is not advancing at a normal rate. After this seven-year period the child will often surprise everyone with his apparently sudden knowledge. The teenager also may suffer from the same opinions of his elders. Reaching the adult stage will provide more acceptance, for he will then be respected as a genius or someone with tremendous potential for success. This unique level is a learning process through which you may contact your past and manifest your knowledge in this lifetime.

SPIRITUAL LEVEL: $Y=7$

The capacity of this Level depends on your approach to the conditions of life. Retaining a positive attitude is the secret to this "Y" Level. You will feel negativity strongly and be tempted to react the same way. The lesson here is to understand how and why people relate to one another and how the negative system of energies motivates rejection. The child will respond to these circumstances quietly, but as an adult you may react in such a way as to lose your balance. Inner control and strength must be maintained. Avoid confrontations and focus on the light. Through this positive approach you may receive much wisdom which can be used for the benefit of others. Writing, teaching and invention are controlled on this seven-year Level.

SPIRITUAL LEVEL: H=8

The Physical Level of EIGHT dominates the Spiritual Level. This is not to say that spirituality does not exist during this eight-year period. You will be focused on material things, which the "H" can help to analyze. Insecure needs surface and the "H" requires recognition of them on an earthly level. This vibratory frequence is like the perfume of a flower, not the flower itself! Seeing how you can gain, improve and progress without hurting others will be made clear during these eight years. The roots of this Level are effective, for they color and determine the results of success. It is essentially an adult Level, although children may become demanding as they go through their childhood and teen years. The EIGHT influence can bring in what is needed if control is monitored and filtered through this Spiritual "H" Level.

SPIRITUAL LEVEL: Q=8

All ages experience a need to be successful. You'll see people constantly striving toward proving themselves in many situations. Having failed to achieve something fully in a past life, they now feel this urge to excel. As long as the need is moderate all will be well. When it becomes excessive the Spiritual "Q" can cause you to be unthinking and relentless in trying to achieve your goals. A constant driving force will change the lifestyle of all those who experience this particular Level, regardless of age. This eight-year period allows you to experience all the various stages of development. During the last two calendar years of this period you should reach a satisfactory level of success, providing it is through your personal endevors and not at the expense of others.

SPIRITUAL LEVEL: Z=8

The essence of cleverness adds sparks to the Spiritual "Z." Careful control will be required to avoid manipulating others. This vibratory energy can provide a great deal of success which if utilized and not abused may create a brilliant eight-year period. The benefits earned on this Level depend entirely on the methods employed. Through the

13th Transition children on this Level will be leaders. Command is important and allows the child to exercise his mind. As an adult you may demonstrate too much power and frighten others away. Tread lightly and command positions will come your way. Remember, there are *no short cuts* to the level of success you desire.

Spiritual Level: I = 9

This unusual Level is motivated by inner research and long-term planning, accompanied by step-by-step procedures toward a future goal that will involve many. This nine-year period can completely change your spiritual outlook. During this time you will undergo many changes: old relationships will end and new ones be established. The intensity of this level is not felt by the child. Not until the 20th Transition year does this vibratory effect occur. Travel or a change of residence is often the first sign of activity on this Level. A need to explore and experiment can result in new areas of discovery. As the vibration becomes stronger, so does the urge to replace the old with the new.

Spiritual Level: R = 9

Here we see the Spiritual "R" in its most beneficial position. Only through trial and error will you receive the reward of this Level. You'll experience challenge and change, resulting in progress, through the desire to experience spirituality. Like the "I," this is an adult vibration which becomes effective only from the 19th Transition year on. Karma is your companion through this nine-year period. You'll come face to face with past group-karma situations. You must learn from them and walk on! Your adventures will be broad and your answers will come through your experiences. The Spiritual "R" will see you finish your nine-year period greatly educated and eager to share your wisdom.

THE MATRIX

Spectrum Level 5, the MATRIX, contains the TOTALS of the three Levels above it: Physical, Emotional and Spiritual. If there is no middle name, the Matrix is the total of only Lines 2 and 4.

Your skill in interpretation here lies in understanding that the Matrix total for each year governs all the Levels it contains. This total is the KEY that indicates the method of approach for each year. As we look at Peter's example,* we see that in his first year (actually, 0–year one) we have:

LINE 1: AGE   = O
LINE 2: FIRST NAME   = P =   7
LINE 3: MIDDLE NAME   = P =   7
LINE 4: LAST NAME   = C =   3
LINE 5: MATRIX   =   17 =8

Therefore, the vibratory force of EIGHT will govern his first year and continue to be his Key until his third year. At that time his Key changes and becomes TWO. Then, at the age of 7, it once again becomes THREE. This lasts for only one year, then his Key changes to FIVE in his eighth year. For years 9 through 11, he has a Matrix Total of FOUR, which at age 12 becomes a Matrix of ONE for two years. Then at age 14 he has a Matrix Total of NINE for five years. This takes Peter through his 18th year. At the age of 19 his Key becomes the Master Vibration of *22.

Now here's a quick analysis of Peter's first 27 years.:

AGE		MATRIX TOTAL
Birth–2	=	8
3– 6	=	2
7– 8	=	3
8– 9	=	5
9–11	=	4
12–13	=	1

*See Spectrum Block chart on page 97.

AGE		MATRIX TOTAL
14–18	=	9
19–20	=	*22
20–21	=	1
21–22	=	4
22–23	=	6
23–27	=	1

The Matrix Total, then, is the Key that shows you *how* to direct the combination of Physical, Emotional and Spiritual vibrations that occur each year. The Matrix indicates the manner in which the Spectrum Levels can be interpreted.

Analyzing the Spectrum Levels

The first step is to analyze the three Spectrum Levels (Lines 2, 3 and 4 on the Spectrum Block) separately. Consider the nature of the NUMBER and the nature of the LEVEL. Then, for added depth, consider the Matrix Total, which is the Key.

From birth through his second year, Peter was under the influence of the PHYSICAL LEVEL "P." Surrounded by his brothers and sisters he quickly responded to their attention. He learned to express feelings at a very early age. He would smile and laugh when entertained and demonstrate his disapproval plainly with a loud "No!" It was important for him to have short periods alone, during which he would lie quietly in his crib, looking around him. He enjoyed color and music during these quiet times. His eagerness to talk frustrated him and led him to speak at an early age.

The Emotional Level of "P" was recognized in his desire to have stories read to him before he began to talk. I remember his sister Deborah reading his favorite books to him. He would be very adamant about which book he wanted, although he was not speaking then. We had a feeling he could say anything he pleased, but was not yet ready to honor us with this ability. This feeling was reinforced when he did learn to speak quite fluently over a very short period.

Peter's Spiritual Level of "C" was demonstrated in his early love for music. He had his own radio and indicated his favorite stations before he was three. His contentment was evident, as he liked to portray what he felt while listening to music by using paint, chalk or crayons.

His Matrix Total of EIGHT was the family influence, with each of his brothers and sisters playing with him and giving him attention. He loved new toys, especially cars. He enjoyed his quiet times, but also delighted in the boisterous playtimes.

During Peter's third year he showed an enjoyment of learning and developed a quieter personality. I chose not to send him to Kindergarten and decided to prepare him for Grade School myself. I could see that he was not ready for a classroom experience; he was very much into his Matrix of TWO.

When he did register for school, his Matrix of THREE was evident; he could read the newspaper and he was ready to express himself in the world! The change in his Matrix Total from TWO to THREE provided the outgoing aspect he needed to communicate more openly. He had obviously enjoyed his Matrix TWO, but he was now ready to enjoy his THREE in the First Grade.

Following the Spectrum Block can show you the pattern of expected activity. I remember once reading an autobiography in which the author had given specific dates. It was fascinating to see how her Spectrum Block corresponded exactly—except for one section! Later this author became one of my clients and I asked about this particular area in which she had not related activities that the Spectrum Block revealed. She told me that certain events that had happened during a three-year period didn't seem to her to be of particular interest, so she had decided not to include that episode in her book. Nevertheless, the Spectrum Block clearly showed the pattern of events that had occurred then, relating to her Emotional Level.

Each of the Level vibrations can be checked with all the Original Level Aspects for advanced interpretation. When they correspond they indicate activity in that particular O Level Aspect. This gives you a running calendar that can indicate when any of the O Level Aspects will be dominant.

If the Matrix Total corresponds with the O Level Aspects, it's important to maintain a balance among the three Spectrum Levels that comprise its total. If this balance can be maintained, it will indicate a tremendous surge of beneficial energy for your client.

Work with your own Chart; compile your own Spectrum Block. See for yourself how precise and unique this delineation procedure can be. I have found that working with the Spectrum Levels can often reveal memories long forgotten, especially of the early years.

Consider the Personal Life Cycles and how they correspond to the three Spectrum Levels and the Matrix Totals. When the numbers are identical they indicate additional energy in that numerical frequency.

Once you have mastered the Spectrum Block, your skills as a Consultant will be enormously enhanced and your ability to help your clients will increase tremendously. Remember, every effort you make is good. When it is made to coincide and harmonize with pertinent Cycles and Aspects, you can expect full and abundant results.

CHAPTER 9

COMPATIBILITY

In this chapter we'll investigate the fascinating study of compatibility delineation. Everyone is interested in who he or she might be compatible with, whether they are looking for a romantic relationship, a business partner, or just a friend.

There are many questions relating to compatibility. But before you can seriously delve into this study, you *must* have completed the basic Natal Chart of all parties concerned. These Charts must be fully and accurately delineated. In addition, you should have:

1. A good sound knowledge of basic Gnothology to this point.

2. Adequate time to study and compare the Charts.

3. A graph pad and pencil for compatibility delineation.

4. A note pad on which to make notes and record your conclusions.

It's interesting to realize that you and everyone around you respond in some way to the numerical vibrations of *everything* in your environment that has a given name. How much more so then do you react to one another!

LIFELINES OF COMPATIBILITY

One of the most important factors that affects our compatibility with one another is the PERSONAL LIFE CYCLE. This Cycle affects the highs and lows in every relationship to a remarkable degree. Knowing the other person's PLC can help enormously in maintaining a good rapport and in knowing when a little understanding on your part could ease an unpleasant situation between you.

The PLCs can be thought of as Lifelines of Compatibility, because of the noticeable force of energy they contribute to a relationship, either in a positive or negative manner. Understanding the fluctuating energies of the PLCs is the secret of maintaining a successful relationship.

Because of the enormous impact the PLCs have on our daily lives, I tend to think of them as the *primary* compatibility factor. Regardless of the Natal Chart Aspects, which of course gives you excellent insight into basic characteristics, you cannot overlook the fact that all that we are at any one time is governed by the influence of the Personal Life Cycle. It is, then, *a vital Key to the personality*. When you learn as much about this Key and how to use it as you can, you will be able to achieve compatibility and mutual understanding with those you admire and love.

Regretfully, many opportunities for compatibility are lost because the PLC influence is either ignored or misunderstood. For example, say a client was attempting to establish a small business during a PLC of TWO. He could be heading for disaster unless he had the support of a compatible partner. Yet this same client might very well succeed on his own in the same business venture if he attempted it during a PLC of EIGHT!

It is fruitless to work against the rhythms of PLCs. Each year we are meant to experience the ebb and flow of these esoteric Cycles. So your job as Consultant is to design a course of action for your client in accordance with the rhythms of his PLCs.

At birth a baby is born into a Personal Life Cycle that we refer to as the ORIGINAL PLAN (OP). His second year brings him a PLC with the next highest number. For example, if he was born with an OP of SIX, he will be influenced by a PLC of SEVEN during year 2. His third year will display the bombastic energy of the EIGHT, and so on throughout life.

Consider all the vibrational levels that the PLCs bring. Which would be the best year for you to enter a university? to take a new job? to get married? Not all PLCs are conducive to study, employment or marriage, so it behooves you to gain a thorough knowledge of the nature of each PLC. Compatibility aspects are many, but you have to learn which ones are right for what you wish to do and who you wish to do it with. The PLC is the Key to everything you are—and are not.

In the following section you will find *all* the combinations of PLCs listed and interpreted. This will serve as a helpful reference in matters of compatibility. In order to find your current compatible PLC, look for the section with your present PLC. Say it's TWO: look for "PERSONAL LIFE CYCLE TWO"; then look through the following PLC interpretations for ONE through *THIRTY-THREE to find the one most suitable to your own.

PERSONAL LIFE CYCLE ONE

With a PLC of ONE

Two ONES require a lot of give and take. Don't try to compete with each other. Try to plan and decide who will do what ahead of time in any particular situation. You could develop an excellent rapport, so that both of you will feel a large measure of satisfaction. But only one of you should take the initiative at any one time. Be prepared to take a back seat now and then and allow the other to express the individuality of the ONE PLC.

With a PLC of TWO

This is a good combination: one can take the lead and present plans and ideas, while the other will enjoy working and bringing them to fruition. There should be no animosity between a ONE and a TWO PLC; it's an ideal combination for partnerships, marriages, friendships or any joint venture.

With a PLC of THREE

Here's another good combination! The originality of the ONE PLC combined with the personality of THREE allow sufficient expression for both of you. Learn to understand each other's motivations and you will make a great team!

With a PLC of FOUR

The security of the FOUR PLC will accelerate the need of ONE. This can work out well if ONE shows patience. FOUR will want to attend to every detail that ONE originates. Because of the need of FOUR to be exact, ONE will have a tendency to push ahead in life.

With a PLC of FIVE

Let the ONE PLC concentrate on the planning. Don't interfere! If the original plans are well established, the FIVE PLC will enjoy expressing them with flair and possible success. ONE should not allow the ego to play any part in what could be a sparkling relationship.

With a PLC of SIX

The SIX PLC is not accommodating to the PLC of ONE unless the relationship is kept on a social or cultural level. If ONE and SIX are closely related, then ONE should avoid demanding his own way, even if it seems justified. Concentrate on the relationship from a personal point of view and avoid confrontations regarding your abilities.

With a PLC of SEVEN

This is a powerful combination. Don't make personal demands on each other and all will be fine. Each of you will have very definite points of view; if they are used correctly much can be gained, especially in business finances. Respect each other and the combination of the PLC of ONE with the PLC of SEVEN can be quite rewarding.

With a PLC of EIGHT

The robust EIGHT PLC is not into unrealistic goals and dreams. The PLC of ONE must refine his ideas before sharing them with EIGHT. Each of you may be tempted to go in opposite directions with exactly the same goal! Attitude counts with this powerful combination. Tolerance and detailed planning will keep you in harmony.

With a PLC of NINE

The PLC of ONE governs this relationship. As long as the ONE recognizes the sensitivity of NINE this can be an ideal relationship. Both egos are involved quite strongly here. There should be a mutual admiration between you. Respect each other for the qualities you have. Don't disregard the needs that each of you have.

With a PLC of *ELEVEN

The PLC of *11 may demonstrate a parental attitude toward the vivacious PLC of ONE. ONE can benefit in many ways from the Master energy of the *11. Allow the support and sensitivity of *11 to guide you. During the *11 Cycle many are gifted with intuition and can see around the bend in the road of life. Opposites can very definitely attract in this combination.

With a PLC of *TWENTY-TWO

Difficulties could arise in this relationship unless the PLC of ONE is willing to take less of the limelight! ONE feels that he is right and the PLC of *22 *knows* that he is right. So someone has to give! Approached with good common sense, this could be a dynamite relationship!

With a PLC of *THIRTY-THREE

In this relationship the PLC of ONE must be willing to change hats occasionally. The reason being that the PLC of *33 will experience shifts in emotional energy. One minute he will be in command, the next withdrawn, moody and argumentative. Skilful handling is required. ONE can guide *33 into a very successful period if he uses caution and provides the empathy and understanding needed to deal with the EMV of *33.

PERSONAL LIFE CYCLE TWO

With a PLC of ONE

Compatibility between the PLC of TWO and the PLC of ONE is very good. You must ignore the tendency of the ONE to become irritated when he feels his individuality is being challenged! Be supportive, for as TWO, you are the one to complete the ideas of ONE. Be willing to listen to his ideas and be cooperative and sympathetic. You will have many opportunities to bring the ideas to fruition.

With a PLC of TWO

Here is a unique balance of energies—the perfect pair! There should be no problem understanding each other. Keep the relationship equal and give respect and support. This is an ideal situation for partnerships of any kind, as mutual goals can be joyfully achieved with the TWO-on-TWO relationship. Be open and honest with each other and you will both attain a high level of happiness.

With a PLC of THREE

The expressive PLC of THREE should let the PLC of TWO take the lead! The personality of THREE can be quite forceful, so use it wisely. Don't overshadow TWO and all will be well. Allow TWO to offer ideas and lead the way. THREE should feel secure and realize that the outgoing vibrations of the THREE PLC will provide all the exposure needed. Avoid feelings of resentment and enjoy the THREE.

With a PLC of FOUR

The PLC of FOUR is the solid foundation of this relationship. Be content to bring your ideas to maturity. Be open to suggestions from the PLC of TWO, for they will complement your plans. Domestic situations can be warm and satisfactory. Together you will be able to accomplish goals and provide new vision for the future.

With a PLC of FIVE

This is an exciting combination of energies! There could be many highs and lows because of the high frequency of vibrations. If the PLC of FIVE will submit to the leadership of TWO, then you can have a unique relationship. You will need to express all that you are and be complimented for doing so. As long as the final decision appears to originate from TWO it will be fine. Avoid arguments.

With a PLC of SIX

Listen to the PLC of TWO during your SIX year! I have seen excellent and profitable relationships with this combination. When TWO speaks—SIX should listen well, for it is you, the SIX, who has the power to manifest the ideas of TWO. It's a good year to establish any business relationship. Look for an increase in financial prosperity.

With a PLC of SEVEN

The PLC of SEVEN has the opportunity to realize his ambitions. Dreams that have been stored away in the subconscious can actually manifest through the input of the PLC of TWO. Although there may be a tendency to withdraw from each other, this does not mean a lack of understanding. Give each other room to express your feelings. This is a fine combination: develop and apply your sensitivity toward a common goal.

With a PLC of EIGHT

Friendship should be the solid base of this combination. Your outgoing personalities should be ideal for true success, with money, business and fun all rolled into one! Don't take advantage of each other. There should be an excellent understanding between the PLCs of TWO and EIGHT. Reach for the sky and work hard and you will both profit from the energies you invest.

With a PLC of NINE

Here is a beautiful and unusual combination, providing perfect trust between the PLCs of TWO and NINE. NINE has a deeper under-standing of where to go, so let him do the driving! But TWO will also know of wonderful places. Don't be afraid to dream, for with this combination, dreams can come true. TWO and NINE have places to go together!

With a PLC of *ELEVEN

A twin feeling surrounds this combination. One PLC feels for the other. A turning point exists between these two sensitive PLCs—a mutual respect and appreciation. Or it could be just the opposite! Either way, emotions are extreme. If the PLC of TWO recognizes just how far to go and avoids stepping on toes, the PLC of *11 will respond with support and love.

With a PLC of *TWENTY-TWO

If the PLC of TWO can allow the PLC of *22 to get on with his business, there will be little or no problem in this relationship. The *22 has places to go, people to see. He can often appear to be unthinking and unfeeling, but this is not true. The *22 needs the support that TWO can give. Don't look for appreciation, for it is already there. Know you are needed and you'll share the success *22 is seeking.

With a PLC of *THIRTY-THREE

Think of a movie! The *star* is the *33 and the *director* is the TWO. What a wonderful combination! If these two PLCs try to exchange roles, then trouble will arise. Much can be achieved with this blend of Cycle energy. Let it work for you both and be willing to be successful. Once you begin to disagree, you'll waste valuable time in trying to make up. Use the energy to your best advantage.

PERSONAL LIFE CYCLE THREE

With a PLC of ONE

When the PLC of THREE and the PLC of ONE come together, there is a tremendous impact of energy! This energy should be used wisely and not wasted by undertaking too big a venture. One step at a time will accomplish your joint plans. Ideas originating with ONE and activated by THREE will create a prosperous vibratory pattern that spells success!

With a PLC of TWO

Each partner in this exacting relationship can go full speed ahead! Neither ego will suffer. With each partner contributing his own brand of talent they can produce outstanding results. The PLC of TWO should not be demanding and the PLC of THREE should cultivate patience. Serious ventures with a splash of originality should be considered. This team has lots of tempo, good companionship and empathy for each other.

With a PLC of THREE

Two THREES are like two peas in a pod! They are attracted by each other's personality, talent and creativity. Many ideas will flood into this relationship, so take the time to sit down and discover what you can contribute to each other. Personal expression is vital, and through a joint effort each can stimulate the other. Home and educational projects are an excellent focal point during this period.

With a PLC of FOUR

Tread carefully, PLC of THREE! If you don't curb your ideas you're liable to step on FOUR's toes. Here are two extremes of personality that could possibly work well if there is acceptance on both parts. Impatience and tempers will not solve the differences; tolerance is needed for balance. The PLC of THREE must have room for expression; the PLC of FOUR must have space to build foundations.

With a PLC of FIVE

This is a complementary but highly electric combination of energies. The PLCs of THREE and FIVE are highly charged! It is important to plan well before putting things into action. A tendency to be careless can delay your joint activities. Both these PLC levels have insight into the needs of others. Working for and with other people may be rewarding. Avoid emotional outbursts; listen to each other.

With a PLC of SIX

The balance of these two PLCs has a give-and-take quality. Calm discussion and patient planning bring satisfactory results. There's no sense of urgency; a great feeling of contentment flows between them. SIX will have no problem with the expressive THREE. In turn, THREE will thoroughly enjoy the sense of balance and harmony projected by SIX. There is plenty of opportunity if these two PLCs work together.

With a PLC of SEVEN

Certainly a karmic connection exists between the THREE PLC and the PLC of SEVEN! Life has brought you together at this time to motivate each other and accomplish your karmic goals, whether personal, business or creative. You are together for a very good reason. Inspire each other, share your knowledge and talents and I'm sure you'll benefit greatly from your efforts.

With a PLC of EIGHT

This could be a highly successful relationship. The PLC of THREE has every opportunity to shine! The solid of PLC of EIGHT can give positive support to the unusual abilities of THREE. Let EIGHT do the planning. Each of these PLCs ignite the other! The union can be most beneficial financially and emotionally. Don't look back but believe in each other and move forward with confidence.

With a PLC of NINE

There's no shortage of ideas here! Instead, there's clear vision and enjoyment of what might be! The PLC of THREE loves to listen to the extensive ideas of the PLC of NINE. Together they are capable of creating dreams, but may spend too much time doing this. Allow NINE to lead the way. Compatibility between these two PLCs is very good. If NINE can let go of the past he will be successful. THREE must not stand in his way.

With a PLC of *ELEVEN

The PLC of *11 has the vision to see the talents of the PLC of THREE quite clearly. With this vision *11 will also have the desire to offer guidance. THREE may encounter some difficulty with this relationship unless he is prepared to listen and respect the sensitivity of *11. They are the absolute opposite in approach, yet can be ideal as a team. Each should recognize and respect the other's potential.

With a PLC of *TWENTY-TWO

The PLC of THREE is capable of dealing with the strength of the PLC of *22. He can achieve this by being himself, with no pretence. The PLC of *22 has the opportunity of channelling his Master energy through the THREE PLC. This will result in success for both. The intelligence of THREE will find a source of inspiration in the powerful Master energies of *22.

With a PLC of *THIRTY-THREE

This is possibly one of the greatest of all PLC combinations! If each PLC is at his best, there is every chance for brilliant success. If ideas and plans are firm there should be no hesitation in going forward. "Completion" is the keyword, after solid initial foundations. The energy flowing between these two PLCs is derived from a Cabalistic root which esoteric scholars consider to be most beneficial.

PERSONAL LIFE CYCLE FOUR

With a PLC of ONE

Try not to get upset at the strong influence of the PLC of ONE. You march to a different drummer! By listening to his original ideas you may very well provide the right answers. Your stability is like a rock and the ONE will sometimes lean a little on your strength. Once you develop and acknowledge what you have to give each other, you will enjoy bringing your sensible ideas to fruition, and so will ONE.

With a PLC of TWO

Good companionship is the basis of this relationship. You should experience easy, comfortable feelings with no hidden resentment and have a clear and refreshing attitude toward the same goals. TWO can fill your need to prepare for the future. You can offer the stability and confidence the TWO needs to promote himself. You are both affected by your surroundings: quiet places, gardens, the countryside and home help to bond you together.

With a PLC of THREE

Form a relationship with a THREE PLC and you could have a friend forever! Your basic need to get to the bottom of things will be complemented by THREE, for he needs what you have to offer. You'll appreciate the success you can share. Interests in the fields of research or medicine or any esoteric areas will be energized through your connection with THREE.

With a PLC of FOUR

From the Tree of Knowledge the karmic fruit is offered to this fortunate combination. Here at last is the ideal time and opportunity to solidify ideas. This lifetime now offers the first step toward reaching your earthly karmic goals. Exciting possibilities await if both FOURS will exert the right kind of energy for each other. This means a special kind of achievement. No procrastination, please!

With a PLC of FIVE

Many interests are shared by these two PLCs. There are many situations you will enjoy. However, the PLC of FIVE will want to skim over areas that you feel need more detail. Insist on seeing the full picture before exerting any energy and you will receive respect and cooperation from FIVE. Overlook the natural inclination to escape inward. Let the vivacious FIVE PLC bring out the best in you.

With a PLC of SIX

Your first reaction to the PLC of SIX is not always the best! However, if you work together you can both be more than satisfied. Your natural inclination is to "do it alone." The SIX may feel it necessary to supervise or disagree with your basic requirements, but if you both agree not to disagree you can easily experience an unusual and exciting chain of events. Do it your way and smile; SIX will smile back.

With a PLC of SEVEN

Another interesting karmic aspect is formed in this relationship. It requires hard work on your part, but the PLC of SEVEN will share the load. Follow your natural inclinations but allow SEVEN to express his feelings. The joint input could result in a very interesting venture. Make sure that you finish: completion is necessary for whatever project you undertake.

With a PLC of EIGHT

This is a robust combination. Thoughts and actions are geared toward material success. Don't feel overshadowed by the PLC of EIGHT. This would be a foolish waste of valuable time. Instead, concentrate your energies on a common goal, for it could be extremely rewarding. A relationship established between these PLCs inevitably will last a lifetime. Keep your sense of humor and you'll be able to laugh all the way to the bank.

With a PLC of NINE

These two PLCs exhibit extreme differences in approach. If each PLC can recognize this fact then it can result in an excellent relationship. You will deal with the rudiments and the PLC of NINE will be looking far ahead. The natural tendency for NINE is to have long-distance vision. You concentrate more on how to start. The road between can be enlightening, for you can learn much from each other.

With a PLC of *ELEVEN

You two will appreciate and sympathize with each other. This can be a sensitive relationship that is protective and stable. Promote your basic plans and let the PLC of *11 enlarge upon them. You may have to take a different approach to life because *11 can easily accept your protective vibrations to support his vision. This will do no harm and you'll feel gratified to be of real service.

With a PLC of *TWENTY-TWO

A cycle of success is imminent for the joint energies of these two PLCs. The year will appear to go by quickly, so be sure you activate and release any resistance on your part. The PLC of *22 can make rapid progress if his path is clear. Unique and profitable ideas can manifest if you both respect each other's input. Leading roles are available in the exciting drama this year can bring!

With a PLC of *THIRTY-THREE

You may feel uncomfortable with the persistance of the PLC of *33. This is unlike your way of doing things. You'll hear yourself saying, "It's not what he does, but *how* he does it." Yet this is just a karmic test: if you succeed you will both share the rewards! Rid yourself of ego and keep silent, firm control. Be ready to take the reins if *33 becomes exasperated. Together you'll experience new and original concepts and achieve unexpected success.

PERSONAL LIFE CYCLE FIVE

With a PLC of ONE

Equality is essential! Don't leave home without it! Mutual respect must be the basis of this relationship, otherwise you will become competitive. The PLC of ONE has very positive ideas and he usually thinks them out well. Your versatility could be the vital link needed to achieve your joint goals. Mercury will energize this link between you. Your outgoing personalities will add color and you'll score high marks socially.

With a PLC of TWO

This relationship will require work! You must be the one to take the initiative, otherwise the PLC of TWO may become disinterested. You will feel no magnetism drawing you back to square one! TWO will rely on you to take the lead. You'll be required to monitor the energy of the FIVE so that TWO doesn't feel cut off by your far-reaching vision. Pull in your horns and all will be well.

With a PLC of THREE

This can be an invigorating partnership! Reach for the stars but be consistent with each other. Have confidence and share your ideas; you have much to offer each other. Your level of understanding can be excellent. The PLC of THREE can successfully demonstrate your joint endeavors. Establish a bond of trust and you can have an outstanding relationship.

With a PLC of FOUR

A PLC of FOUR will be attracted to your vibrant energy like a moth to a light. Try to encourage FOUR to apply his practical abilities to ideas you have conceived. Knowing who is best at what can be the key to your relationship. Each one learning from the other can be a turning point on your life paths. Be considerate and FOUR will return a lifelong loyalty.

With a PLC of FIVE

With this coupling of energies, you may think you're in "earthquake country." Periodically someone is going to blow off steam, although not necessarily with each other. If this does happen the relationship is bound to suffer. Actually, if both FIVES are balanced the vibratory energy fluctuating between them can be used for something dynamic.

With a PLC of SIX

When the PLCs of FIVE and SIX are brought together a wonderful energy is generated which stimulates the intellect! Acting upon their initiative this pair of PLCs can reach the heights of success. If they work as a team and share every detail, I can't see how they could avoid success. FIVE constantly motivates SIX; the result is seen in the reaction of SIX, who can analyze and maintain correct levels of energy.

With a PLC of SEVEN

The PLC of SEVEN has the vibratory level to tone down the PLC of FIVE. This can have a therapeutic effect on FIVE. It's doubtful that being constantly close will work! As long as there is occasional distance between them they can have a rewarding relationship. The electric energy of FIVE will force SEVEN to retreat inward, which is good for SEVEN but not for FIVE.

With a PLC of EIGHT

Success is inevitable if you are prepared to heed the practical advice of the PLC of EIGHT. This may be difficult for you, but nevertheless it could be profitable! EIGHT will enjoy the challenge of organizing your talent. You may feel restricted and somewhat overpowered at times, but with your sparkling personality it will not be apparent.

With a PLC of NINE

The PLC of NINE allows you to express exactly who you are and how you feel! A wonderful sense of freedom exists between you and NINE. This elasticity gives you both plenty of room for personal expression. NINE will provide the vision and you'll contribute your versatility. Keep things on the light side and you'll also share a wonderful sense of humor.

With a PLC of *ELEVEN

It will take a great deal of effort to communicate with the PLC of *11. The ponderings and depths of the *11 will not attract your effervescent personality. If your shared interests are studying and/or philosophy, then you have a good basis for spontaneous discussion. Otherwise, finding common ground may be difficult.

With a PLC of *TWENTY-TWO

Follow the wisdom of the PLC of *22 and you will go a long way. The *22 PLC will quickly recognize your true potential. Take the time to listen and learn. Your Cycle energy is readily understood and accepted by this Master *22. Be open to suggestions and be willing to accept some form of regimentation. The Master vibratory energy of *22 will put everything in order.

With a PLC of *THIRTY-THREE

Your partnership with the PLC of *33 indicates that destiny has brought you together for a special achievement! This could be personal, material or spiritual. Your karmic paths are now merging for a specific purpose. It is now time to complete an unfinished karmic situation. Through understanding and sensitivity you'll recognize a special bond between you. Let your FIVE guide you toward your purpose.

PERSONAL LIFE CYCLE SIX

With a PLC of ONE

A feeling of confidence flows between you and the PLC of ONE. Your steady vibrations give ONE a sense of stability. Your shoulder can get quite wet with ONE's tears of frustration. Your inner strength is vital and you will gain the harmony and balance you need through your empathy and understanding. If decisions are made for any venture, be sure that you personally supervise the itinerary.

With a PLC of TWO

You will enjoy companionship and pursuing joint efforts. The vibratory force between you will bring much pleasure into your lives.

This year can be a busy one, with lots of activity and long talks discussing future plans. State your ideas regarding stability and finance, and TWO will have much to offer.

With a PLC of THREE

This will be a close and long-lasting relationship. The element of satisfaction will always be there. You'll have much to share and yet you two are very different in personality. The similarity stems from your natural ability to accept the ways of the PLC of THREE. Often THREES are quite insecure and will need you there to lend a hand and speak a kind word. Although your personality is not so extroverted, your PLCs will blend beautifully.

With a PLC of FOUR

A strong, reliable force holds these PLCs firmly together. Hard work, study and loyalty will bond you, and you'll feel comfortable with the PLC of FOUR. You'll feel secure in the certainty that working together will bring you results. FOUR will appreciate your strength. You may have to give it often.

With a PLC of FIVE

This is an important connection, with a karmic purpose! You will be the one to analyze and evaluate. Listen to the PLC of FIVE and the variety of ideas presented. The contrast in your vibratory Cycles reminds me of an eclipse! You will unfold and realize how close your karmic goals are in this special relationship. As you join in a common cause you will create unusual beauty for all to see.

With a PLC of SIX

Highs and lows are well accommodated in your association with the PLC of SIX. Like the musical scale, you can create harmony and will be a mirror reflection of each other. Your moods and temperament will not cause disharmony. In this relationship your depths reach serious levels for serious endeavors.

With a PLC of SEVEN

A good place to start this relationship is at the beginning! Unless you do this you'll feel confined and suffocated by the vibratory level of the PLC of SEVEN. You may have a great attraction for each other, but I suggest that, like medicine, you take it in small doses. Give and take is essential on both sides to make this relationship work.

With a PLC of EIGHT

A third party is needed for this relationship! You two are all talk and no action. You are the planners, but it may very well stop right there! You may enjoy each other's company, and excitement will appear to be everywhere, but it won't materialize quickly. Your sense of stability will be challenged by the expectations and bravura attitude of EIGHT.

With a PLC of NINE

This is a wonderful year for marriage or for establishing any other kind of permanent relationship. Your karmic cycle, like a clock, is now at the point where it is going to chime! There will be a promise kept and karma to complete. This is a perfect year to solidify the past, appreciate everything to date and continue to learn the lessons of life with joy.

With a PLC of *ELEVEN

The Wheel of Fortune is ready for you to spin! Be sensitive to the PLC of *11. The balance needed must come from you. Being afraid or holding back will not spin the wheel! Be cooperative and open with your thoughts and feelings. The *11 PLC will always be ready to listen. Never allow your partner to sink into a depressed mood; be ready to uplift him.

With a PLC of *TWENTY-TWO

This blending of personalities can create a magnificent team! All that the PLC *22 is capable of being he is willing to share with you. Curtail extravagance, supervise the finances and you'll bring out the best in *22. Don't be afraid to stand your ground. The *22 PLC is just a teddy bear under your vibratory influence.

With a PLC of *THIRTY-THREE

This is a winning team without a doubt. Both of you may be impossible to understand, and those around you may have difficulty keeping pace with your future plans, but let nothing deter you from your goals. Allow the PLC of *33 to plan the moves and you keep the faith and act as the ambassador. The *33 PLC will take the bull by the horns. Be alert to each other's needs.

PERSONAL LIFE CYCLE SEVEN

With a PLC of ONE

You may receive many opportunities through the PLC of ONE. It will necessitate your input to trigger this action. Ignore your natural tendency to withdraw. Volunteer your opinion—it will be greatly appreciated. You are respected and must make the effort to contribute whatever ONE is looking for. Although you dislike the stage, now is the time to perform!

With a PLC of TWO

This will be a peaceful relationship, with no interference from the PLC of TWO. You make no demands on each other and have a mutual respect for each other's privacy. Even a joint sabbatical would be successful. TWO is an ideal companion for you this year, but not for romance. This will be a strong, silent bond which allows you both to pursue your individual interests. TWO will be a source of inspiration for you.

With a PLC of THREE

Congratulations, PLC SEVEN, you have just been awarded a "live wire"! Yes, you do have the time and you will benefit from this relationship. All that THREE has to offer can motivate your own personal aspirations. You'll discover aspects of his personality that you find refreshing. Just take time out now and then for your own solitude.

With a PLC of FOUR

Your ideas will be well handled by the PLC of FOUR. This is a good time to join forces and achieve some profitable results. Give FOUR all the time he needs to put these plans into action. Watch the drawing board as FOUR works hard to produce your talented creations. FOUR will offer the fullest cooperation.

With a PLC of FIVE

Patience is required. The PLC of FIVE may encounter difficulty in keeping within the boundaries of discipline you need. Take time off to be alone, concentrate on your goals. This is the year for you to produce results. FIVE is attracted to the depths but can be distracted. Focus on your work and this will inspire the eager FIVE. Respect your personal needs and plumb your depths.

With a PLC of SIX

Look before you leap! The PLC of SIX will go overboard if you give him too much space. Your need to express yourself through work will make SIX step in and reprimand you. This situation can become unpleasant, so try to avoid confrontation. You can accomplish this by not responding to any friction. SIX needs and seeks balance. Your power of concentration will not appear balanced to him.

With a PLC of SEVEN

This can be a very satisfactory relationship. The peaceful atmosphere will be quite inspiring. Long hours will give you all the time you need for self-satisfaction. But you must avoid self-pity. If either of you is feeling down I suggest that you take the time to talk it out. Otherwise, depression can halt all progress. Do not commiserate together!

With a PLC of EIGHT

Behind the scenes you are a genius! Your inspiration can spur the PLC of EIGHT to great heights. Your support is essential and will be required often. Give it and you'll enjoy the robust vibration of the EIGHT. You won't be expected to do more than your share. EIGHT will enjoy helping you experience satisfaction and rewards.

With a PLC of NINE

Two great minds think alike! Karmic satisfaction and the knowledge that all is well exists between you and the PLC of NINE. Few words are needed between you, for you share a great depth of understanding which was initiated in a previous lifetime. You are hungry for knowledge and eager to learn. Your vibratory levels are most compatible.

With a PLC of *ELEVEN

This is a special year! Perhaps you'll both find what you're looking for. The time is right for you to be in touch with your Higher Selves. There is work to do and it should be accomplished by your joint efforts this year. This will be a year to remember and a year to forget the past. You enhance each other with vibrations that come together in a positive way.

With a PLC of *TWENTY-TWO

If you support the PLC of *22 you'll enjoy taking a quiet role in the success of this Master vibration. Your participation is vital to the *22, so don't run away! It is time for you to be recognized and to preview your long-term success. The *22 PLC will delight you as he generates the Master energy. Feel it, enjoy it and don't resist.

With a PLC of *THIRTY-THREE

I cannot recommend this relationship, unless you are willing to be subservient to the powerful needs of the PLC *33. It will be a waste of time to try to reshape the ego of *33. On the other hand, you can enjoy the association if you decide not to take everything too seriously. Be tolerant and just let it happen.

PERSONAL LIFE CYCLE EIGHT

With a PLC of ONE

Together you can accomplish great things! If coming from opposite directions you can be devastating. Work with the PLC of ONE and you will succeed beyond the average. You both have powerful PLCs; together they provide an excellent level for achievement and business. If you don't get along with each other, leave well enough alone!

With a PLC of TWO

In this relationship there are no sparks flying! You must be the one to forge ahead. The PLC of TWO will be right behind, giving support and cooperation. This is a low-key but exciting combination. TWO will be loyal to your cause and contribute good common sense but you must be the one to instigate activity.

With a PLC of THREE

This is a vitalizing mixture of energetic vibrations. What a team! You may have your ups and downs, but there is sufficient empathy between you to eliminate any serious pitfalls. If you have something special on your list to achieve, this year could be good and uplifting. You must be ready to give support when THREE is feeling low; of course it has to work the other way, too.

With a PLC of FOUR

You have similar basic ideals, so this can be a solid relationship. The PLC of FOUR will be a great source of strength. You will be the extrovert in presenting your joint goals to the world. FOUR will be content to allow you to do this as long as you stick to the plans you made with each other. FOUR will keep it all together and is no less ambitious than you. Your outgoing energies will help you promote your joint cause.

With a PLC of FIVE

Here are two extrovert forces. Working at the same time can be chaotic! Fun relationships will thrive. Business relationships *must* be reasonable. There must be a lot of give and take, and if you allocate separate responsibilities you'll be an unbeatable team! Avoid stepping on each other's toes and all will be well. Many goals can be set and achieved.

With a PLC of SIX

You can actually magnify your vibratory level with the PLC of SIX. This unique blending of forces is complementary. THE PLC of SIX is sensitive and forever trying to balance the books, so don't forget to acknowledge his cooperation. Don't rock the boat. Give him full recognition for his efforts. If you let SIX present your ideas, it will be done in a concise and sensitive manner.

With a PLC of SEVEN

The PLC of SEVEN has a clear, brilliant outlook. Ideas and future plans can be perfected with this team. There is quite a difference in approach, yet your two opposite energy levels create an exciting vibration for achievement. Working together can be a karmic experience, fulfilling and rewarding on a very basic level.

With a PLC of EIGHT

The coming together of these identical PLCs is a repeat of a past karmic experience! You both have what is needed during this time in your lives to establish your success. But you must forget your egos. This is no time to waste this very special union. The power must be shared and not fought over, for this is a karmic situation that can be wonderful for you both.

With a PLC of NINE

When the PLCs of EIGHT and NINE join forces the impact provides an excellent opportunity to achieve unusual levels of success especially in specific areas of humanitarianism. This is the time to follow your star and throw off useless restrictions. Allow the NINE to motivate your talents toward new fields of endeavor. It's breakthrough time.

With a PLC of *ELEVEN

Try to analyze your relationship. There is a purpose to it; if you will listen to your inner voice you will discover great new avenues to travel. The PLC of *11 has the answers! It will require patience on your part to stand still long enough to appreciate the depth of the *11. This could be your year to experiment and promote yourself. You may be the missing link for *11!

With a PLC of *TWENTY-TWO

Batman and Robin are old hat: this duo is Batman and Batman! Many opportunities will be presented this year. Your energies are electric. Don't waste them. This is a rare situation in which karma once again invites you to share your purpose, with a promise of success. Much strength is available through your joint energies, but if your minds are not working in unison you could very well fly off in different directions.

With a PLC of *THIRTY-THREE

Concede some of your vibratory power to the PLC of *33. Keep in mind that *33 is actually searching for your type of vibratory influence! You can be the one to lead the way *after* the *33 has explained and expressed himself, become elated and then settled down. Your extrovert power can generate all kinds of possibilities if you remember to allow Master *33 to fully express his whole plan.

PERSONAL LIFE CYCLE NINE

With a PLC of ONE

The PLC of ONE will be attracted to your bubbling inspiration! If you wish to make this partnership work, you must provide the support required by ONE. Go one step beyond dreaming: share your broad views and explain in detail the pictures from your unlimited vision. ONE will respond and help to make them a reality in a trusting friendship.

With a PLC of TWO

The serenity that exists between the PLCs of NINE and TWO is extraordinary! A deep level of understanding and compassion flows through and nourishes this relationship. The energies are directed toward each other, and your outward expression will have a sense of unison. As you look ahead, there will be harmony and close rapport as TWO responds to and supports you splendidly.

With a PLC of THREE

This may appear to be the perfect relationship. The PLC of THREE may seem rather overbearing to your NINE vibration, but you can choose to ignore the personality and concentrate on your potential together. If this happens, you will have to allow THREE to demonstrate his feelings as they arise! Try to be patient and accommodating. Your need to explore will be supported and understood by THREE.

With a PLC of FOUR

Here you have the high and the low, sky and earth! You will want to soar with the eagle, but the PLC of FOUR will have a natural tendency to bring you to earth. This could be the basis of a strong and lasting relationship. There will always be plenty of room for adjustment. To give in halfway provides an exact point of balance. Both of you express your Cycles strongly, but don't worry, it should be fun.

With a PLC of FIVE

With the PLC of FIVE you will lose any sense of restriction as far as letting go and moving on is concerned! Any reluctance on your part will be eliminated by the versatility of the FIVE. You are the one with the vision. FIVE will want to make it a reality. This is another karmic situation. You have met someone who will be happy to see your long-distance vision come into focus.

With a PLC of SIX

Jack and Jill or Samson and Delilah could not be closer! A deep and lasting bond is formed with the combination of these two PLCs. If this relationship doesn't work out, then you have clear evidence of karma at work. It's a wonderful merging of Cycles; there should be much joy and love. You have much to give to each other.

With a PLC of SEVEN

Here the intellect blends and many plans can be put into action. All levels of human emotion will seem similar, which provides a perfect balance for mutual understanding. Your ability to look to the future will be needed. SEVEN may not see things exactly the same way, but with your support he can be taught to do so.

With a PLC of EIGHT

This is a "dessert" relationship: too much will create too many calories; a little at a time can be beneficial. You must both have room to be expressive within your own Cycles. Each of you has a vital ingredient to give the other, but to go beyond this point is trespassing. You can be close without total absorbtion in each other. You can enjoy high-key activity, but you also need to take time to relax.

With a PLC of NINE

Destiny has brought you together for very positive karmic reasons! Use this time and Cycle well. You are deeply rooted into the past, with exciting visions of the future. There is no sense of competition, just a beautiful blending of ideas, talents and initiative. Don't procrastinate, for you both have the opportunity of enjoying not only companionship but meaningful activities together.

With a PLC of *ELEVEN

First I would say listen to the PLC of *11. If you experience any difficulty in reaching your goals, then *11 will have the answers. Be sure to use your Cycle energy to its fullest extent. Rid yourself of any barriers you have erected in the past. The *11 PLC may offer you a warning now and then; listen and then make a decision based on your joint input. Tranquility is the gift you give each other.

With a PLC of *TWENTY-TWO

The PLC of *22 will automatically be attracted to your NINE energy. This attraction should provide opportunity. You will have the vision, *22 will have the know-how. With a team like this you can achieve the heights. Don't feel overshadowed by *22. With your combination of energies, the lion becomes a pussycat.

With a PLC of *THIRTY-THREE

This is a coming together to complete past karmic endeavors! It is a magnificent time in your lives to delve into your subconscious levels and take up where you left off. As you develop a new level of understanding you will appreciate and value the energy you give each other. Keep your thoughts and actions positive and with this perfect partnership you can enjoy the fruits of your karmic labor.

PERSONAL LIFE CYCLE *ELEVEN

With a PLC of ONE

A karmic situation exists here in which you may feel a sense of responsibility toward the PLC of ONE. You will have much to offer. Share your intuitive feelings regarding his projects. Your caring and helpful attitude will be greatly appreciated eventually. Remember, his vision is not as far-reaching as yours; although he appears inspired he needs your interest and guidance.

With a PLC of TWO

This can be a quality relationship endowed with long-lasting respect. Shared interests and talents can surface and become prosperous. Ideas will mingle, and it will be difficult to decide whose idea it was in the beginning. This will be a sensitive, caring year in which karmic energies bring you face to face. A positive outlook is needed; negativity can only destroy what was meant to be beautiful.

With a PLC of THREE

You will see the PLC of THREE venture into areas that make you feel unsettled. In your wisdom you want to prevent any deliberate or accidental mistakes, but if you interfere THREE will become obstinate, which can make things worse. Just be there in case mistakes do happen! THREE is attracted to the wisdom of Master Vibration *11, although it may not appear that way. Your loyalty and strength can do wonders.

With a PLC of FOUR

A year of solid foundations can be the result of this relationship if each of you listens to the other. Support and hard work will be rewarding. It's a good year to plan and save and help each other achieve your goals. Tremendous strength surges between these two Cycles and patience comes easy. Plans that materialize from this combination are truly outstanding.

With a PLC of FIVE

If the PLC of FIVE thinks you are trying to stabilize his activity, he'll run as far as he can! With your Master *11 you can find subtle ways to cooperate with the extroverted FIVE. Look for the very best potential, then encourage FIVE to use it. Too much supervision or apparent control will make him look in other directions. What you have to offer is good. Try not to be too critical.

With a PLC of SIX

Your natural inclination will be to retreat from situations that are controversial. The PLC of SIX likes to find the balance between extremes. Let him do this, and you concentrate on your mutual interests. You are a valuable asset to this relationship. Your depth of understanding will encourage SIX to take the plunge. You may wince once in a while, but this is necessary for great success.

With a PLC of SEVEN

Your Cycles work well together! You will be the point of motivation. When you exert your Cycle influence the PLC of SEVEN will respond and share his philosophy and intentions. Don't attempt to dislodge his foundations, otherwise he may retreat into the woodwork. Encourage him, give him confidence when needed. Be a good shoulder to lean on and SEVEN will reward you with the results of his hibernation.

With a PLC of EIGHT

The PLC of EIGHT will listen to your ideas. Think things out, be methodical and the result will be enjoyable if not profitable. Don't be put off by what appears to be a dominant personality. EIGHT has a loyal and steadfast Cycle which is compatible with the Master *11 energy pattern. Consider yourself the planner and EIGHT the doer and you can reach the pinnacle of success.

With a PLC of NINE

Unusual ideas result in unique results! Perfect harmony can exist between you. As NINE is inclined to project forward, you are able to provide him with what he needs. Be prepared for when NINE resists the force of change. Your constant encouragement will be needed, but you'll be happy with the results. This could become a profound relationship.

With a PLC of *ELEVEN

You two have much to gain from each other! There's so much to share and enjoy. These two Master Vibrations will form a nucleus of energy that can initiate a great deal of power. This is ideal for large-scale planning. This year is the perfect time to make serious decisions and achieve abundance. You will spend much time alone before you put your brilliant plans into action.

With a PLC of *TWENTY-TWO

Master minds at work! With your Master levels you should instantly recognize the skills and needs of each other. Put these ideas together and you will have a Master Plan. Although you may be tempted to get out there and do it, leave action to *22 while you generate more ideas. Expand on your plans and be ready for success.

With a PLC of *THIRTY-THREE

This is another Cycle combination comprised of Master Levels that has the fullest potential. Knowledge is powerful and when combined can create and materialize Master Plans. This is the year to give it all you've got! As separate individuals you inspire others; as a team you can lead yourselves and others to success. *33 is the vehicle—*11 is the wheel.

PERSONAL LIFE CYCLE *TWENTY-TWO

With a PLC of ONE

This relationship could be excellent; on the other hand, it could also be frustrating! It depends entirely on the attitude you have toward the outgoing PLC of ONE. If you allow him to express his individuality he will return a deep sense of loyalty. ONE needs to sense his own security, regardless of whether or not *you* are his security! As long as you know you are the focal point of this team, all will be well.

With a PLC of TWO

A crossroads of complementary vibrations merge into this relationship: people listening to people, sharing ideas and emotions. Harmony can prevail when both PLCs equally contribute positive vibrations. The Master *22 is tthe dominant leader, yet TWO contributes energy that brings out these leadership qualities.

With a PLC of THREE

Your Master vibratory power can motivate the PLC of THREE to achieve brilliant results! There is good chemistry for a close working relationship. Work concentrated in fields of research (including Gnothology) can be very rewarding. Keep your sights high, for the sky's the limit. I have seen very positive results with this combination of PLCs. Use it well and you'll make your dreams come true.

With a PLC of FOUR

Go for it! From a positive angle you can produce exactly what you desire. The only obstacle I see would be the inability to aspire to the Master Level and use it fully. You have what it takes, so take it! The PLC of FOUR has the key to your energy cycle. Allow him to use it and you will have not only success but the true satisfaction of karma fulfilled.

With a PLC of FIVE

If you have a compatible interests, all will be fine. If not, you won't be attracted by the flair of the FIVE. Your need to organize things will be met with opposition from FIVE *unless* he has an interest in what you're planning. This is important for working together. On a social basis you can have a substantial friendship, even a close, loving relationship.

With a PLC of SIX

On the road of Destiny, life offers you the chance to share your Master *22 with the PLC of SIX. For it is only by sharing that you will realize the impact of this energy level. A karmic situation yet to be completed exists between you. Together you have outstanding strength and can reap the rewards being offered. Doing it alone and disregarding SIX's contribution will limit the results.

With a PLC of SEVEN

When the PLC of SEVEN associates with your Master energies he is motivated to create original and outstanding work. Obviously, you were meant to be together at this time! Mutual respect and trust will bring about originality. SEVEN will thrive on your input: there will be a constant drive toward achieving joint goals. Give each other the respect and trust you require.

With a PLC of EIGHT

The word "flamboyant" comes to mind when I visualize the Master *22 associating with the PLC of EIGHT. This can be a vivid and colorful partnership. You'll be able to scale the heights yet still have a pleasant relationship. Again you have a karmic influence that suggests an excellent opportunity in this life for overwhelming success. Time goes by quickly, so don't waste one precious minute during this year.

With a PLC of NINE

The PLC of NINE can be exactly what you need to put your ideas into practice. You'll be a great working team, for you'll find that NINE is capable of interpreting your original concepts. The frequency of your joint vibratory level has its own esoteric source. There is much to learn and share, with an outstanding tolerance level. If you need groundwork, you must either do it yourself or find another person for the job.

With a PLC of *ELEVEN

Establish what each of you has to accomplish. Hard work will prove worthwhile. Be alert to the needs of the sensitive *11. A demanding attitude on your part will only serve to close up *11 completely. Give compliments whenever necessary and be patient. The contribution from *11 will be well worth waiting for. When it comes to your turn—you can run with it!

With a PLC of *TWENTY-TWO

You will both be concerned with people. Together you make outstanding leaders in whatever category you prefer. When you see the Statue of Liberty do you look at the torch or Miss Liberty herself? When you focus on the identical Cycle of *22 with *22 you must see the *whole picture*. This can only be accomplished by the mutual confidence of both partners concerned.

With a PLC of *THIRTY-THREE

This relationship can go off like a bomb at any time! Here you see the Master energies being forced to merge and present a new and original concept of life. Some plans are made in heaven. Perhaps this relationship can be considered like that. A pact was made by these two souls; now is the time to manifest it. The result can be powerful and spiritual.

PERSONAL LIFE CYCLE *THIRTY-THREE

With a PLC of ONE

No one needs to feel threatened in this relationship. Each of you play entirely different roles. You are the power and the PLC of ONE is the instrument of expression. It is your original concept that ONE will feel he must express. Let him do this as you continue to prepare the blueprints behind the scene. You should discover your purpose this year and enjoy the opportunity of bringing it into the light.

With a PLC of TWO

Rewards will be earned this year, especially if you have been working toward certain goals. The PLC of TWO is the ideal partner in any business proposition. Your vibratory level is high: ideas flow and you have a special energy that can be used along with the intuitive skills of TWO. The contribution from TWO is the ability to tune into your needs and provide successful groundwork.

With a PLC of THREE

This is a year of mental filing and reconsideration of past goals. With the cooperation of the PLC of THREE you'll be able to gain much clarity. Let your thoughts flow and take time to discuss the details with him. THREE will rely on you for this type of input. Together you may touch into unusual and fascinating projects. It could be an exciting year, so enjoy!

With a PLC of FOUR

This will be a challenging relationship! It's ideal for new and original concepts. Concentrate and work together, with each of you aiming for the same goals. This could be a year of hard work, but this should cause no tension unless you create waves. Ambitious projects can be initiated; your keen sense of perfection will be respected by FOUR. Probe, research, discover facts; now is the time.

With a PLC of FIVE

As you direct energy into this relationship you'll receive back all you need! The PLC of FIVE can work well with this combination. Your input encourages the positive aspect of FIVE. Your influence will trigger his intellect, and the result will be originality plus swift-moving decisions. FIVE acts like a tonic for the powerful *33.

With a PLC of SIX

This can be a deep and sensitive relationship. You will enjoy the serious aspect of each other. Knowing how each other feels, sharing the highs and lows, will come quite naturally. Avoid feeling down for any length of time. You are the one with the Master energy, so use it to encourage and uplift. This is a constructive relationship which can produce exactly the results you need.

With a PLC of SEVEN

Meeting each other at the top would not work! Your personalities are completely opposite and so are your interests. Someone would have to give in, and that's not easy for either of you. On the other hand, if you start at the beginning of a project your joint energies can be terrific. This is because you will willingly share knowledge to get the show on the road.

With a PLC of EIGHT

Grand ideas and great plans may be all just talk! Before you see any worthwhile action you'll have to take command by allowing the PLC of EIGHT to think and do. Your position will be to observe and offer guidance whenever necessary. Trust plays a big part in this relationship. If you can take the right roles, you can have a very good year with each other.

With a PLC of NINE

This is a karmic relationship full of understanding. You are able to anticipate each other's needs, for this is a solid relationship that has lasted through time. You'll enjoy new places and experiences that will awaken past memories. Contentment and harmony are the gifts shared between *33 and NINE. Use them well and try not to take advantage of each other.

With a PLC of *ELEVEN

The power of these two Cycles merging can change your lives! It is an extreme type of relationship. Together you can achieve the highest goals. You are gifted and can give each other exactly what you need. On a grand scale you are an outstanding team. On the personal level you are somewhat different and apt to quarrel at the least provocation. But like the children you soon kiss and make up.

With a PLC of *TWENTY-TWO

You are like two heads of state! Each time you meet you feel the need to discuss your own policies. If the powers decide to join forces things can happen. Yet a sense of reluctance lingers. In your wisdom you are both hesitant to totally submit, yet you learn a lot from each other. It's almost a battle of wits, competitive but fun. Put your minds together and stop playing games.

With a PLC of *THIRTY-THREE

You are like two peas in a pod! Identical vibrations create a unique Master Level. Nothing can stop you from attaining the success you want except yourselves! The only thing missing from this strong Cycle relationship is a sense of humor. Remember that life is far too important to be so serious. Try not to be victims, for you are leaders at heart. Many will rely on you; don't let them down.

INCOMPATIBILITY

As you use the foregoing Compatibility Guides, you'll see that they are written in a positive manner overall. But you must learn to use your carefully developed sensitivities when it comes to interpreting them.

If two people are not operating on a positive level, then you'll see the variations in the uses of their Cycles. When you recognize the exact opposite in behavior patterns between a couple, you'll know that these clients are operating on the negative aspects of the Cycles. You'll also see most people fluctuating between positive and negative attitudes. This is normal.

In counseling, therefore, it's a good idea to point out the wonderful possibilities available to the clients during any one Cycle period. Stress that the choice of *how* to use the energies is always up to them, and that there is no need for them to remain stifled by the Cycle vibrations. Show them how they can work toward the best potential use of their energies. Warn them that by continuing to activate only the negative aspects they can destroy all chance of attaining the best that the current Cycles are now offering.

Master Cycles are easily misued and the opportunities lost due to lack of knowledge. Negative Master Vibrations will expose you to depressed and argumentative clients who can't get along with other people. Through sensitive counseling and the impartation of knowledge, you can help such a client begin to change for the better almost immediately.

Working with your Cycles is imperative. Children are so open and innocent that you can watch them play for five minutes and recognize what Cycle they are experiencing. Adults can also be this way; some are constantly trying to disguise their true feelings, but their real emotions are easily seen by the trained Gnothologist. If they continue to hide their true selves from the world, eventually the energies of their Cycles turn inward, where they can cause self-destructive behavior patterns or illness. The results can be devastating!

The important thing to remember is that a good Consultant knows the power of Cycles, understands their positive and negative uses and is skilled at recognizing them at work in his client's Natal Chart.

CHAPTER 10

GRIDDING

GRIDS are used to delineate information regarding compatibility between people. It's a convenient method of presenting the information in a concise, easy-to-read manner and eliminates the need for continuous cross-referencing of Charts.

There are four basic types of Grids. The first three can accommodate any number of people, while the fourth is intended for two people only.

1. Relationship Grid (RG)
2. Family Grid (FG)
3. Business Grid (BG)
4. Lunar Grid (LG)

Grids can provide a complete picture of a specific group of people in a close relationship, whether it be friendship, family, business or romantic. The first three types of Grid can be as large as you wish or small enough for only two people. The size and depth of the Grid is determined by the amount and type of information you desire about the people concerned. A complex Grid can include every Aspect in the Chart! A complete Chart has complete information; the same goes for the Grid. And don't forget that you'll need to update the Grid, just as you do the Chart, according to changes in Cycles and Aspects.

In the chart that follows, I have given two examples of Grids—a Family Gird and a Lunar Grid. The procedures for setting up a Relationship or Business Grid are exactly the same as for the Family Grid shown. I have included five people, with 35 Aspects from their Charts. You may use more or less.

175

Gridding

When making a Grid for Family, Business or Relationship you may elect to use any number of Aspects you feel necessary for the consultation or research. The Gridding procedure is identical for all three Grids. For this example I have used basic Natal Aspects.

Family Grid.	O	O	O	I	2	C H	V	S C O	K K A	L L L L	L K K	P P P
	S	P	E	P	E	I V	M	T V O	O K A	T T O O	O O R	K P E
	P	Y	K	T	B	P	T	C O C	E A T	O O O O	O R K	S E L
								6 P₁ P₂ P₃	1 2 3	P₁ P₂ P₃ P₄ B₁ B₂ B₃ B₄	R₁ S	P Y K C

Person A	22	5	7	3	11	6	1	3	5	11 5 11	6 6 7	4 11 3 22 5 9 3
Person B	5	9	5	33	3	9	6	3	11	3 11 5	22 11 9	2 1 7 8 4 8
Person C	3	7	2	7	4	8	5	2	2	3 6 1	6 5 11	3 5 1 7 8 3
Person D	5	11	5	7	3	5	11	1	8	3 1 7 3	11 22 33 1	3 2 3 5 11 5 1
Person E	5	3	8	5	8	9	7	22	1	5 4 1 8 1	8 3 4 8	4 2 6 6 1 5 8 8 9

Lunar Grid: Male = Prt 3   Female = Prt 6 = Compatible Prt.

	Jan.	Feb.	Mar.	Apr.	May	Jun.	Jul.	Aug.	Sep.	NTW
Male —→	4	5	6	7	8	9	1	11	3	X
Female —→	7	8	9	1	11	3	4	5	6	X
	11	4	6							

male = ①   ④ = female

(13)

= Joint effort = Esoteric Balancing Tool = ④ EBT.

Grids.

Family	✓
Business	✓
Relationship	✓
Lunar	✓

PROCEDURES FOR THE RELATIONSHIP/FAMILY/ BUSINESS GRID

1. Allow sufficient time to compile and delineate the Grid from the Natal Charts.

2. Natal Charts must be checked before compiling a Grid; they must be up to date and exact.

3. Have enough note paper to write down your observations. Each person in the Grid should have their own separate sheet of paper to avoid confusion. Also keep a separate reference sheet to write down your general comments and observations.

4. Remember that opposites—odd and even vibrations—may either complement or detract from each other.

5. When presented with incompatible numbers, examine the Rootings, which will show why they are not compatible. Although you may see similar Rootings, two people may have difficulty in seeing the same situation in the same way. Their points of view and deep-seated principles may differ on an identical Rooting digit or in a digit that is considered incompatible.

6. Numbers in Gridding are like the spots on dice: it depends on how they fall.

7. If the Original Soul Prints (OSP) and Original Expressive Keys (OEK) are identical, this relationship is karmic and the people involved are meant to complete or achieve some joint venture.

8. If the OSP and Present Soul Print (PSP) are identical, the nature of the karmic plan is emphasized and solidified but remains unchanged.

9. In a marital situation, if the woman's OSP is identical to her Present Expressive Key (PEK), this indicates that she is expressing what her partner desires on a karmic level.

10. When two people have identical Original Plans (OP), it means that these plans were determined prior to birth and that in this life they will share an experience that is essential to their progress here on earth. If the Rootings *and* OPs are

identical, it suggests that they have been very close in a previous life.

11. Locating and comparing a FIVE vibration with a THREE expands the nature and interpretation of the FIVE, which becomes endowed with wisdom *only* in that relationship.

12. Karmic Planning means that when any of the following Aspects are matched as listed below, the two souls concerned have previously planned their contact here on earth. An analysis of each individual Chart will reveal the purpose for this meeting.

OSP = OSP

OSP = OEK

OSP = PSP

OSP = PEK

This prearrangement may involve karmic debts to stabilize an imbalance between two souls. Or one may have chosen to help the other accomplish a particular purpose. The reason for the connection on this level is unknown; we only know that they have come together to solve a karmic situation, good, bad or neutral

13. When completing a Grid, enter the *present ages* of the people listed in the column marked "PA" (Present Age).

MUTUAL GRID VIBRATIONS

MUTUAL GRID VIBRATIONS (MGV) are used *only* when working with Grids. Regardless of the present status of a relationship, whenever you discover identical vibrations for the same Aspects, such as:

OSP 4 = OSP 4

OEK 9 = OEK 9

and so on, you will find that this number (or numbers) becomes very helpful in dealing with any problems in the relationship.

MGVs indicate a link to future possibilities. Relationships that are strained or experiencing difficulties can find hope through the MGV. This identical vibratory pattern has become distorted between the parties involved, much like a rope may become twisted. But you'll discover that relationships that appear to be unrepairable may not in fact be severed! Any negative feelings that exist and have existed for a period of years may be caused by this "twisted" MGV. If so, there is every possibility of healing the wound.

Both parties are operating from the identical vibratory pattern. By analyzing the positions of both you'll see that one of them has taken the *positive* aspect of the digit while the other has taken its *negative* aspect. Good counseling can encourage one or the other to adjust their opinions and feelings to the *center point* of the vibration. In doing this they will obtain a much better perspective on the situation troubling them. If they can be made to work with the balance of their identical vibration, they may eventually find their way back to compatibility. You should also try to determine *how* both parties ventured into the negative and positive aspects which caused the problem.

THE LUNAR GRID

Not all relationships are well established, nor have they existed for a number of years. Clients may consider a new relationship important as they contemplate future plans, whether romantic or business partner is concerned. The next few months may be crucial. "What can we expect from each other?" "Will we continue on our present path with the same understanding we now share?" "How can I approach her again after what I said?" These are a few of the typical questions you may be asked, so you should be prepared with a knowledge of the various Aspects and Cycles that will assist in the consultation.

Here's where the LUNAR GRID comes into play. It is a simple Grid which, through the use of the ESOTERIC BALANCING TOOL (EBT),* can anticipate the development of the relationship in question. The EBT will offer a detailed analysis of the approach required during any one calendar month.

*Refer back to Chapter 3, Procedure 52, pp. 49–52.

The Lunar Grid can accomodate any two people: male and female, two females or two males. In the example on the chart I have completed a Lunar Graph for a male and a female. Their PLCs are THREE and SIX respectively, which indicates a compatibility for the year. Their Individual Monthly Cycles (IMC) are displayed for a nine-month period. By adding the two IMCs you arrive at a total which immediately reflects the expected conditions of the relationship for any one calendar month.

If the resulting number is a single number such as FOUR, FIVE, EIGHT, etc., you will find a strong base of understanding between the two parties. This number becomes the EBT.

If the resulting total of both IMCs is a double-digit number (such as the 13 in the example), extra Rooting is required:

$$5 + 8 = 13 = 1 + 3 = 4 \text{ EBT}$$

The ONE will be the approach of the *first person* in the Lunar Grid. The THREE will be allocated to the *second person*. Thus, this delineation would indicate that Party #1 (the male) will, under the influence of his FIVE IMC, form an individual attitude toward achieving the required FOUR for mutual satisfaction with his partner. Party #2 (the female) would, under the influences of her EIGHT IMC, be outspoken and active in achieving the FOUR EBT.

Here's another example: Let's say that a male has a FOUR IMC for January and his female partner has the same IMC for that month.

$$4 + 4 = 8$$

You know immediately that there is a deep understanding between them during this month. Each of them, experiencing the identical IMC, will be able to participate in producing a joint EIGHT vibratory level. This would be wonderful if they were planning to get married or begin a business partnership this month. It is strongly indicated that they have finished their initial planning and that by joint effort they could produce excellent results during this month.

One final example: You have a female with a THREE IMC and a male with a TWO IMC, both in August.

$$3 + 2 = 5$$

The resulting FIVE EBT shows that Party #2 (the male) will be very supportive of Party #1 (the female). As she is already experiencing the vibrant energy of the THREE, with the support and joint energy of the FIVE they can share a very exciting August, whatever they undertake.

Use the Lunar Grid whenever you have a question about the possibilities and suggested courses of action between any two people during any one month. It's excellent for joint business ventures, applications and interviews for employment, major decisions, family relationships (one person at a time), and of course, for romance!

As you establish your clientele and after the Basic Natal Chart is complete, you will inevitably get into areas of decision-making and relationships. It is advisable to have a Lunar Grid on file along with each Basic Chart.

THE ESOTERIC BALANCING TOOL

The EBT is an extraordinary Key to delineation in depth when used with the Lunar Grid. It immediately shows how each party is feeling his own energy level and how by combining those levels the two can create a unique force of its own for them to work with.

The EBT is ultimately derived from the Personal Life Cycles (PLC), which originate in the Christ Cycle (CC). Cycles reveal our personal energy patterns as they stem from the Universal Pattern. As all vibratory frequencies emanate from One Source, we can recognize one another's needs by understanding and making use of these frequencies, which are the Universe's gift to us.

The PLC, then, determines the manner in which the subsidiary Cycles react within its influence. So it's important to realize that each IMC is colored by its governing PLC. Success arises from the proper understanding and use of these energies as a whole, from Universal to IMC and IDC.

CHAPTER 11

MEDITATING ON YOUR ASPECTS

Once you have completed your Gnothology Chart and have become thoroughly familiar with the numbers, Cycles, Transition, etc., you are ready to approach the depths of the study of numbers.

Numbers are more than strokes of pencil or ink on paper—they are vortexes of energy which you must experience on a deeper level. As with all knowledge, you must come to recognize the two approaches to them: the EXOTERIC, or outer, path and the ESOTERIC, or inner. You are the master of your own destiny, yet you are compelled to follow your Original Plan, for you yourself chose it before you were born.

You enter your esoteric journey through your birth date and experience volumes of color caused by your personal impact through the heavens to earth. Your soul qualities are magnetized to the energies of gems and crystals. The forces of the planetary cycles keep you disciplined within the earth cycles you must complete in order to follow your karmic path, which is forever woven into the tapestry of life after life.

You may endeavor to apply various kinds of divination to your daily life—Astrology, the Tarot, Runes, Gnothology, etc.—but it is essential that you come to understand that there is a SPIRITUAL aspect to each of these studies. In Gnothology, I refer to this spiritual dimension as the KETHER FACET.

THE KETHER FACET

Approaching the depths of the numerical Cycles you pass through the various levels that compose each number until you arrive at the Cabalistic center. Examining the KETHER FACET you will see that in addition to a positive and negative aspect, each number has a covert, esoteric side to its nature. This third interpretation—the SPIRITUAL —is governed by the Covert Law of Numerical Sequence. Within this law is demonstrated the LAW OF CAUSE AND EFFECT, one of the basic laws of the Universe. To learn and understand this Cabalistic principle, you must turn to the Key of meditation, for through this inner discipline you can enter the esoteric depths of the numerical world and find the means to quench your yearning for spiritual knowledge.

The knowledge of this THIRD interpretation of numbers provides a three-dimensional view of the Natal Chart. THREE is the Triad, the Trinity, the number of Completion. To enter this phase of your study, meditation will allow you to pass beyond the physical and mental confines of your Chart. Once you begin this procedure you will never think of a number as just a number again!

MEDITATION ON THE ORIGINAL PLAN

Meditating on a particular numerical Aspect can be exhilarating. As you progress, you will want to meditate on all of the Aspects in your Chart, for you can gain different insights through each of them. Once you have entered the world of each one through meditation, you will see the true light of your destiny.

Choose an Aspect for which you would like guidance and insight. An ideal place to start is with the ORIGINAL PLAN (OP). Complete the normal preparation procedures for meditation (see: Vol. I, Chapter 14, pp. 199–200). Choose your candles, which should be in the *color* that represents your OP number (see: Vol. I, Chapter 6, p. 33, "Balance Scale"). Peter Paul Connolly's OP is TWO, so his candle would be ORANGE. Next, select the *musical note* equivalent to the numerical vibration and color. (Peter would choose the note D.) When you feel you are ready, commence the following procedure:

1. Light one or more candles in your OP color. (The more candles you use, the higher the vibratory level will be.)

2. Concentrating on your Inner Eye, begin to hum the musical note corresponding to your OP color.

3. As you hum, visualize the OP color in your Inner Eye area. Let it become brighter and brighter.

4. As the color becomes brighter it also begins to cover a larger area. As it becomes larger, it becomes a DOOR.

5. Continue the above visualization until you can see a large, solid Door the color of your OP.

6. At this point let your humming gently fade out and focus your attention on the Door.

7. Knock on the Door as many times as the number of your OP (Peter would knock twice).

8. Continue to concentrate on the Door and the OP color. Wait for permission to enter.

9. When you receive permission visualize yourself dressed in a robe of your OP color. Now open the Door and walk in.

10. As you enter in your colored robe, you will see your MASTER seated to your LEFT. Say to him:

    I SINCERELY WISH TO UNDERSTAND MY ORIGINAL PLAN. WITH YOUR GUIDANCE I ASK THAT IT BE MADE CLEAR TO ME.

11. Now listen for his answer and experience the fruits of your meditation.

12. When he has finished talking to you, give thanks to him for his wisdom.

13. Leave through the Door.

14. For a few minutes, rest and contemplate what you have learned.

15. Write down all the information and details you can remember. (If you have a tape recorder, you may prefer to dictate this information into it.)

MEDITATING ON THE OTHER ASPECTS

This form of meditation can be done with any Aspect in your Chart. It will provide you with information that you can use in your everyday life. It will also help to expand your level of consciousness so that you can come to understand and accept your personal destiny.

It's important to make notes after each meditation. Eventually you'll be able to see the whole picture and receive the knowledge you desire.

Meditating on individual Aspects will alert your higher levels of consciousness to bring together all that you are and wish to be. These meditations are quite beautiful and open up areas of consciousness that may have been dormant. Your whole life will be enhanced and spiritually uplifted after these experiences.

Be patient with yourself and realize that to achieve the level of awareness you are seeking will require time and practice. After years of meditating on my OP I still receive information that is of great value.

Here are some of the other Aspects you may explore through meditation and the type of information you may expect to receive from them:

OSP	will reveal the original formula of purpose.
OPV	will allow you the vision that others see.
OEK	will alert you to your goals here on earth.
OP	will show you your path of destiny.
CO	will give you the Key to achievement.
1ET	will let you see the influence of this structure.
2ET	will release the energy of your OPV.
CSB	will balance any negative vibratory flow.
KOP1	will focus on your individuality.
KOP2	will open up your reserve of energies when needed.
KOP3	will make you aware of past karma.
RE	will present the true Key to your identity.
SV	will instigate the desire to achieve your goals.

AC   will amplify your purpose and provide guidance.

PT   will energize the life force giving you power.

IVP   will expose submerged unused characteristics.

LT POINTS will assist in choosing your direction.

OCG   will enlighten and analyze your efforts.

L.Opps   will motivate you in the right direction.

L.Obs   will remind you of what you must avoid.

PLC   will throw light on your path and give direction.

IMC   will put you on the right track for the month.

IDC   will protect you from making mistakes today.

Enjoy these beautiful meditations. Use the colored candles to harmonize with the Aspect you are meditating upon.

CHAPTER 12

MEDITATIONS ON THE EARTHLY MASTER NUMBERS

In Chapter 14 of Volume I presented a series of meditations on the Basic Numbers ONE through NINE. Now, at this level of your studies, I'd like to give you meditations for the three EARTHLY MASTER NUMBERS (EMVs): *11, *22 and *33.

As you know, these three Master Vibrations form an esoteric bridge between the nine Basic Numbers and the HIGHER MASTER NUMBERS, or HIGHER MASTER VIBRATIONS (HMVs). We'll study the HMVs in the following chapter.

Meditations on the EMVs differ from the meditations for Numbers ONE through NINE: they require a different approach. As you prepare for meditation on these Master Numbers you are in fact preparing to receive higher wisdom and guidance for your life path.

Follow the preparations outlined in Vol. I (Chapter 14, pp. 199–200). Be sure to have a notepad or tape recorder handy. Allow sufficient time to relax and contemplate your experience after the meditation. Be certain you have created a peaceful and relaxed atmosphere for yourself. Unplug or muffle the telephone. Make sure you have sufficient time to do the entire meditation without hurrying.

Meditation on these higher levels requires that you bathe beforehand. The color of your clothing now becomes more important. Wear the colors listed below if possible; if not, then wear white. Whatever type of garment you wear should be loose, flowing and comfortable. Here are the colors assigned to the three EMVs:

1. *ELEVEN   =   Silver or White
2. *TWENTY-TWO   =   Red-Gold or Red and Gold
3. *THIRTY-THREE   =   Sky Blue

You should have at least *three* candles in the color of the number you intend to meditate upon. Your feet should be bare, or you may wear clean white socks or stockings. No shoes. If you have long hair, it should be lifted up or tied back to allow the head chakras to energize and circulate freely.

All jewelry, watches, etc., must be removed except for any piece that vibrates on the desired frequency. Acceptable jewelry would be:

1. *ELEVEN   =   Silver, Platinum or Mother of Pearl
2. *TWENTY-TWO   =   Red Gold or Coral
3. *THIRTY-THREE   =   Lapis Lazuli

The stones must be set in gold, silver or platinum, or they may be worn without a setting of any kind. If you don't have any of the above and you would like to wear something, you may use a clear quartz crystal that has been prepared in the proper way (see: Eileen Connolly, *Tarot: The Handbook for the Journeyman* [North Hollywood: Newcastle, 1987], Chapter 4).

Fast for at least *two hours* prior to meditating. The longer the fast the higher the level you will attain. Do not meditate if you feel hungry or uncomfortable. Concentration is very important, so it's vital that you feel at ease and relaxed.

The meditation procedure for each Master Number varies. I would suggest that you make a tape of the steps of preparation that follow; this will take your mind off the procedure and let you concentrate on the substance of the meditation.*

PREPARATORY MEDITATION FOR THE EMVs

The following steps are designed to lead you slowly and peacefully into the actual meditation on the Master Number you have

---

*I have these meditations recorded on tape. If you would like to purchase them, write to me at the address given at the end of this book.

chosen. The steps are the same for all three numbers. Follow them exactly.

1. Begin by repeating your PERSONAL MANTRA (see: Vol. I, Chapter 6). If you are recording your meditation procedure, then let it begin with your Personal Mantra, which should be played for no less than ELEVEN minutes for any of the three EMV levels.

2. Lie down on your back and as you hear your Personal Mantra, relax your entire body. Your recording will now give the following instructions if prerecorded: they should be spoken *slowly*, allowing you time to follow each instruction easily and in a relaxed manner.

3. Let the weight of your body pull all the negativity down and out of you. Let the earth absorb your physical, mental and spiritual pains. Hear the voice and wisdom of your Higher Self take control now.

4. Visualize a bright WHITE LIGHT above your head. Bring this light down into the top of your head. Feel it circulate and cleanse every living cell in your body. Feel this concentrated white light penetrate your ears. Let it clear all negativity from your eyes. Feel the bright white light now penetrate your eyes and feel its glow radiating from your face.

5. Bring this divine white light down into your throat, feeling it clear and heal as it moves down into your chest. Feel it fill your chest and lungs. See white light bursting into brilliance, cleansing, healing, repairing every living cell. The power builds and now comes to the heart center.

6. The white healing energy now concentrates in the center of your heart. Each breath you breathe distributes this divine healing light into every part of your body. Each breath you inhale cleanses and heals every vital organ in your body. Each breath you exhale releases all negativity. Allow your Higher Self to take control of each incoming breath, focusing the bright white light of divine healing directly on the heart center, distributing the power of your Heavenly Father to every living cell in your body. As your breath is released it carries away all that that is no longer a part of you.

7. As this wonderful healing continues let your Higher Self control the healing process. Your body is your Temple. You are a soul with a body, not a body with a soul. Your Temple is now being cleansed and healed. See the center of your being lit up with white light. Every corner of your Temple is bathed in purity and light. This is now a perfect place for the Holy Spirit to enter.

8. You are now the center of all that is pure. Your body, your Temple, is full of divine light. Lift this light to your Inner Eye and focus on the top of your head. Touch your Higher Self. Let the light be bright within your Temple. Let the flame of acceptance reach from your heart center to your Inner Eye. Let divine wisdom and knowledge now penetrate your consciousness. Feel the flame lighting the way.

9. Bring down the energy to your Emotional Level. Each small chakra opens like a flower as the divine white light touches this sensitive region. Around your middle is a tight belt of emotion. This belt has many chakras. They are small and dark. Now bring the divine white light to the center of this belt. As the light touches the center see the brilliance of the buckle. Beautiful heavenly colors radiate as the belt relaxes. Breathe in deeply. Let the light from your Inner Temple now shine into your Emotional Belt. Become aware of the many brilliant jewels now aglow with the purity of Inner Light. A beautiful relaxed feeling now descends upon you.

10. Let this light relax you. The many chakras around your waist are now bright with new hope and divine light. No longer do you feel the restriction of past deeds, words and doubts. Feel your Inner control take over. Around your waist now is the belt of wisdom, glowing and waiting to be used. Your strength grows, you are feeling the command. You are ready to receive direction.

11. Take one deep divine breath of energy and direct it through all the vital organs within your Inner Temple. Feel it correcting, healing and renewing tired cells. The rejuvenating energies bring light to all areas. Negativity, disease and self-neglect now leave your body with every outgoing breath.

12. Fill your whole body with bright white light. Allow the Higher Self to control the spread of the God energy through your heart center. Each part of your body is being healed as your outgoing breath takes away everything that is detrimental to your existence. Allow the white light to go down into your legs, the pillars of your Inner Temple. Feel the living strength as it sweeps away all negativity. Bring the light into your bloodstream, into your muscles and through your bones. Now feel the white light circulate through your feet. Every toe is an outlet for the release of this energy.

13. You are now drenched in the light of divinity. The Christ is within you. The energy coming from your feet is no longer negative. It is clear bright white light, forming a solid foundation under your feet. Take one divine energy breath, bringing up as much light as possible from the area under your feet, the Malkuth. Lift this energy up, up, up to the top of your head. Now lift it up above your head. See the white light circling around your head like a crown. As you look down your legs are aglow with white light. Your waist is girdled in multi-colored beauty. Your health is perfect. Feel the Christ Light now lift up through your body and feel its divine glow upon your face.

14. You are blessed, you are One, you are Light. Lift up your consciousness now from your Inner Eye to the place above your head. Touch the Crown—the KETHER. Feel your oneness with God and with Light. You are healed, you are Christ-like. With this energy one thought will provide blessings for all those you love. THINK OF THIS. Your next thought will bless all the sick. The light within you will be extended to all those who need this blessing. THINK OF THIS.

15. You are blessed, you are One, you are Light, the Christ Light. Whatever you ask in His name will be given. One thought, one breath and it will be done. THINK OF THIS. Your Inner Temple is now ready for your affirmation. Place it firmly in your mind and SPEAK IT NOW: (Here affirm what you wish for yourself or others.)

16. Your affirmation has been heard and it is done. THINK OF THIS. Slowly reach out your arms in blessing to all those on God's earth who have any need whatsoever. Give of yourself, for you are the Light and can give everything to all. THINK OF THIS.

17. Know that your place is with God. Know that He has provided this place. THINK OF THIS. Let your face smile as the radiance of His almighty blessings pours over you. Feel the golden rain of His blessings. Abundance is all around you. All your needs are now being cared for. You have no needs. THINK OF THIS. Release all that you are to all there is. THINK OF THIS.

18. Give thanks for all that you have. THINK OF THIS. Once again be aware of your Inner Temple. Hear the voice of wisdom speak within. Be still, soul-still, STILL WITH GOD.

19. Come forward into your light. Where you stand and when you speak let there be light. You are light, the Christ Light. This is the everlasting blessing that lives within your Inner Temple. Do not lose sight of this blessing. Keep your faith strong and allow your Heavenly Father to guide your way. Have no fear, for fear is acceptance of negativity. You are loved and as you are loved so shall you love. THINK OF THIS.

20. Make no plans, for they are already made. Rest in bright white light and see with clear new vision the way that has been made for you. THINK OF THIS.

21. Accept all that has been given and know that there is more. The everlasting fountain of life is flowing and waiting for your every desire. THINK OF THIS.

22. In bright white Christ Light repeat these words:

I AM THEE I AM. LET THESE WORDS BE MY LIGHT. LET THESE WORDS BE MY PATH. LET THESE WORDS BLESS ALL THOSE I LOVE. LET THESE WORDS BLESS ALL THOSE IN NEED. LET THESE WORDS HEAL THE SICK. LET THESE WORDS BLESS ALL THAT I AM. I AM THEE I AM.

23. Repeat your Personal Mantra now and visualize your entry into your higher meditation. DO THIS.

24. NOW STEP FORWARD FROM YOUR TEMPLE AND ENTER THE GATE OF THE MASTERS. I will wait here for you. (Now go forward into your EMV meditation on the following pages.)

25. As you return:

    WELCOME. YOU ARE NOW WEARING THE PROTECTIVE ROBE OF PURPLE. MAY IT FREE YOU FROM ALL FUTURE NEGATIVITY. MAY ALL THOSE WHO TOUCH YOU RECEIVE THE DIVINE ESSENCE THAT DWELLS WITHIN YOU.

26. GIVE THANKS. Contemplate your experience. Feel the difference now flowing within you. Write down your experience and keep this record of spiritual growth. Amen.

MEDITATION ON THE *ELEVEN

As your Preparatory Meditation brings you to the Entrance Gate of the *11, step out from within your Inner Temple and wait before the Gate to continue your journey. Observe the Entrance Gate to the *11: it is made of marble with a strong light shining on it which creates a silver and pearl effect. The Gate is studded with many esoteric symbols, each of which is surrounded by mother of pearl. As you wait to enter, examine the symbols. Among them is one for you. Find it; when you recognize it knock THREE times and wait.

The Gate will be opened by your Master. He will greet you by name. Now step through the Entranceway and the Gate will close behind you. Your Master will ask you your purpose. Answer him: "I COME TO DISCOVER AND LEARN MY PURPOSE." The Master will then direct you onto a path. Thank him and begin to walk down the path and experience whatever occurs.

Observe all that you see and hear. If you meet someone on the path you may ask questions and request the person's name. Relax and take your time. Walking on the *11 path gives you insight into your destiny.

When you return to the Entrance Gate, your Master will give you a message and then open the Gate for you. Thank him and repeat the message as the Gate closes behind you. Before opening your eyes, contemplate the message and bring it into your Inner Temple. (Now go back and complete the two final steps on page 195.)

Often your Master will walk with you down your path and give you insight and wisdom regarding your present status in life. Learn all you can from him. This beautiful meditation is inspiring and rewarding. It will comfort you and teach you the true direction of your destiny.

MEDITATION ON THE *TWENTY-TWO

As your Preparatory Meditation brings you to the Entrance Gate of the *22, step out from within your Inner Temple and wait before the Gate to continue your journey. Observe the Entrance Gate to the *22: the sun is shining directly upon it, making it appear covered in fire. It is beautiful and exciting and red-gold vibrations dance upon it like sparks, denoting the energy level of the *22. In the center of the Gate is a magnificent coral plaque upon which are written many names. When you find yours, knock THREE times and wait.

The Gate will be opened by your Master. He will greet you by another name! Step through the Entranceway and the Gate will close behind you. Your Master will ask you how you use your power. Answer him: "I COME TO LEARN MY DESTINY AND HOW TO USE MY POWER." Your Master will then direct you to the Hall of Records. Thank him and feel free to walk into the building which contains the records you wish to consult.

As you enter the Hall of Records you may feel overwhelmed by the seemingly endless shelves of knowledge available. Sometimes your Master will go with you and help you find what you need. Other times you will have to discover it for yourself or ask help from anyone who may be nearby.

When you return to the Entrance Gate, your Master will ask what you have learned. Answer him, relating the information you have discovered. If you have any questions, feel free to ask them. You may also ask him for further guidance. He will then open the Gate for you. Thank him and repeat what you have learned as the Gate closes behind you. Before opening your eyes, contemplate your new knowledge and bring it into your Inner Temple. (Now go back and complete the two final steps on page 195.)

Treasure and record your knowledge. Use it well and soon. To learn more, visit the Hall of Records again, using the correct procedures for the *22 meditation.

MEDITATION ON THE *THIRTY-THREE

As your Preparatory Meditation brings you to the Entrance Gate of the *33, step out from within your Inner Temple and wait before the Gate to continue your journey. You are now released from the confinement of your physical body. As you wait at the Entrance you will feel a beautiful sky-blue cape placed gently about your shoulders. Observe the Entrance Gate to the *33: a warm vibratory glow emanates from the exquisitely made Gate. You will feel a change in temperature as you notice that the Gate is completely encrusted with fiery dark blue sapphires. Each one sends out a divine blue ray. Wait until one of the rays touches you. Then knock THREE times and wait. As you wait to enter feel the healing energies penetrating your whole being. Concentrate on your own personal ray, which is entering your Inner Temple through your heart center.

The Gate will be opened by your Master. He will greet you and give you a name known to no other. Each time you visit him on this *33 level, he will address you by this name. Your Master will ask you what service you give. Answer him: "I HAVE COME TO LEARN OF MY SERVICE, FOR I AM READY TO SERVE." Your Master will then take you to the Cobalt Lake. The surface of this lake reflects the sky. Your Master will ask you to look deep into the lake. As you look its color changes to a wonderful dark cobalt blue. Now you will say: "I AM READY."

The water will now clear and you will see a vision of what you have come to see, whether it be in the past, present or future. Your Master will remain with you and explain anything you need to know about your vision. If there is anything you do not understand, ask for a further vision.

After the vision has vanished and you have asked your Master any questions you may have, he will then return with you to the Gate. Before you leave he will give you a task that must be performed before you return again to the *33 level of meditation. This task is a part of your destiny. It may include a duty to others, a personal obligation you have neglected or a correction in your habits. Whatever he gives you to do you must do, for this is the purpose of the one who seeks service on the *33 level.

Your Master will then open the Gate for you. Thank him and promise to complete the task he has given you as the Gate closes behind you. Before opening your eyes, contemplate your task and bring your service into your Inner Temple. As you place it amid the bright white Christ Light, ask that you be given the strength, courage and dignity to complete this service. (Now go back and complete the two final steps on page 195.)

Your Master stays with you during this meditation. You may speak freely and openly to him. Know that your karma is corrected and that others will benefit from your service on this *33 level. Before beginning this *33 meditation, be sure that you are ready and willing to be of service. "Responsibility" is the keyword on this level. The privilege of entering it in the future depends upon your completing the task assigned.

THE ROLE OF CHOICE

The word "choice" is associated with these Master Levels. Without a doubt they represent choices in your life; they give you a feeling of extremes. You can choose to work toward the positive side of the vibrations and in so doing, reap the rewards the EMVs can bring. Or you can dwell on the negative side and feel a sense of loss and emotional insecurity.

Choice is the issue! When you have EMVs on the Original Level, understand that a Change Level will not remove or reduce the Original EMV vibrations. You can decide to do one of two things:

1. Acknowledge the Original EMVs and work with the Master energies, discovering how they can best be used with your change of name.

2. Ignore the Original EMVs and feel their driving force attempting to penetrate your Present Level, bringing wasted energies and negative results.

The choice is up to you.

EMVs ON THE CHART LEVELS

1. Always delineate the Original Level before proceeding to C or P Levels.

2. Note ALL EMVs on the O Level and interpret their Chart positions. Analyze WHY they appear in the Aspects they do.

3. Make notes at this point BEFORE proceeding to any other Chart Level.

4. As you analyze the Present or Change Levels, refer to your notes about EMVs on the Original Level.

5. This work should be completed prior to your appointment with a client. This will give you time to prepare your findings and get ready to advise your client how he can benefit on his P Level from the EMVs on his O Level. If he fails to benefit from this advice (his choice), he may feel constantly frustrated, spending too much time at his Emotional Level rather than making the progress he would desire.

As I have said before, I strongly suggest that you apply the above directions to your own Chart before attempting others. *Doing* a Chart can be fascinating; *finishing* it, completely and accurately, is what makes a skilled Gnothologist! When you finish a Chart, you will know what it means and how to work with it. You'll understand that the *skill* of interpretation, which can only be developed through hard work and practice, is what helps your client. This is your responsibility as a Consultant.

CHAPTER 13

HIGHER MASTER NUMBERS

Beyond the Basic Number Scale of ONE through NINE and the EMVs *11, *22 and *33, we find the HIGHER MASTER NUMBERS, *six* further numbers which form the Gateway to esoteric computations derived from ancient Cabalistic formulas. We use the code HMV (Higher Master Vibrations) to refer to them. They are:

**FORTY-FOUR

**FIFTY-FIVE

**SIXTY-SIX

**SEVENTY-SEVEN

**EIGHTY-EIGHT

**NINETY-NINE

You can only advance into a study of these Higher Numbers after you have mastered a thorough understanding of Numbers ONE through NINE and EMVs *11, *22 and *33. After you have mastered the HMV of **99 you can then explore the mysteries of Cabalistic formulas for discovering new areas of divination.

KARMA AND THE HMVs

The six HMVs are considered in a different way from the previous twelve numbers you have been working with. Each of those numbers had both a positive and a negative aspect. With HMVs we take another approach. An activated HMV responds only under karmic conditions—when situations from previous lifetimes are re-enacted. If a client is negative and not experiencing harmonious conditions through his own fault, he will be deprived of the qualities of his HMVs. This means that he will not be able to enjoy the karmic advantages the HMVs offer.

These Higher Numbers can work for or against you. They may be supportive or they may create a barrier preventing you from achieving undeserved rewards. Although the reaction of the HMVs may *appear* to be positive and negative, this is not so. This interpretation is only in the attitude of the individual concerned: his attitude at the time the repeated karmic situation occurs imposes its vibrations on the HMV, thus causing an *apparent* positive or negative reaction. Understanding the HMV provides an entirely new perspective on karmic destiny. You should understand that HMVs are *corrective* karmic vibrations, creating results that are activated according to the karmic balance of the person involved, whether deserving or undeserving.

Your personal attitude toward life does not determine whether the HMV is activated, received or not received. The vibratory rate of the HMV is much higher. It is a contstant reminder of past-life efforts and how they relate to your present efforts. HMVs become evident when the present circumstances of relationships in this life are a repeat of circumstances of relationships in a past life. When karma is created there must be a repeat episode in this life for the purpose of correcting and adjusting the individuals' karmic record.

The Karmic Records hold the information until the identical karma is once again presented. This occurs when your life path touches upon challenges, relationships, vocations and experiences similar to those in a previous lifetime.

Karma Owed to Others

When you owe karma to someone else, it will be recorded as an HMV. If this karmic debt is avoided, any advantage or positive result to be found in the Chart will appear to be dormant. This is seen when a well-structured Chart is inactive—when all the Aspects appear to complement one another, yet there is no evidence of Chart activity.

Good Aspects and Cycles cannot function harmoniously unless you are willing to face up to your karmic debts.

It's important to recognize the HMV frequencies in a Chart. Frustration, nearly accomplishing goals, inability to succeed despite talent —these are signposts of the nonrecognition of HMVs. The qualities found in the Natal Chart are sufficient to achieve the Levels indicated. When the Natal Aspects appear to act as hurdles, this may be another sign of an unrecognized HMV. You should make sure that any obvious blockage in a Chart is indeed an HMV and not because the client is out of balance with either his Natal Aspects or present Cycles.

The difference should be clear: when the client is out of synch with the world, the present PLC becomes stagnant and ineffective due to the self-imposed blockage created by ignoring or refusing karmic debts.

A person may be leading an ordinary life and feel balanced, yet every opportunity seems to escape him. Through consultation you may find that he has an unusual desire to help others, even when it doesn't seem to be necessary. You should look carefully at this urge; you will probably find a karmic connection. If this is so, the urge to help should be encouraged and guided into useful paths. This will activate the HMV in a beneficial capacity and open doors to the client that were previously closed to him.

Having a karmic obligation is not a deep secret. When there is a karmic debt to be fulfilled it will be felt! There is a compulsion to give more than is considered normal in a group or single relationship. A constant urge to overcompensate or be submissive in certain circumstances or with a particular person or group is another tell-tale sign of unaccepted karma owed to others.

Another way to tell such a karmic pattern is in analyzing the energies that seem to resist the success of any endeavor or personal venture. When this occurs repeatedly the client is said to be in the KARMIC CYCLE OF RETURN. He will be placed in life situations in which he will be forced to give of himself whether he wishes to or not. The power of this vibration will activate in such a way that he will become aware, sooner or later, of the Karmic Cycle of Return.

Karma Owed to You

When others owe you karmic debts, things may appear just the opposite! Nothing seems to work out right. Obstacles loom up from nowhere. You may feel a sense of restriction, a limitation on your efforts. Personal relationships may be tense and working conditions frustrating. When situations like this occur, you feel locked in and unable to progress. Inevitably, you have karma owed to you!

You have no control over karmic debts owed you; this is totally the responsibility of your debtors. Consequently, you may feel at a loss in many life situations. You may experience the feeling of being locked into a relationship in which you are not in control. You may find yourself being tolerant and accepting behavior patterns that you find most upsetting.

Since you are *not* the debtor, you do not have to remain in such situations. It is possible to wait a lifetime and not be paid off. You are free to extricate yourself from unpleasant circumstances or relationships without fear of karmic consequences. When karma is slow in being paid to you there is no law that says you must wait for payment in full. As a matter of fact, it can often help the situation if you do choose to extricate yourself. If you cannot manage to do this physically, do it on the emotional and mental levels. Once you achieve success on these levels, it may trigger the workings of karma in others. Due to your disconnecting on these levels you are no longer the victim of a replay of past karmic patterns.

LOCATING THE HMVs

As you delineate your Natal Chart, you may see HMV Numbers in certain Aspects before you reduce those Aspects to their final digits. If, for example, you see a 10 = 1 which is preceded by an HMV of **55, identify the **55 by putting a *red line* around its box on the graph and continue to reduce until you arrive at the final digit. This will make all the HMVs in your Chart stand out boldly and be easy to locate. Each HMV holds karmic knowledge and is telling you that you will undergo a karmic experience in reference to the Aspect in which it appears. There will be a reoccurrence of a past-life experience involving the same souls.

Remember that HMVs are neither good nor bad; they simply indicate where a replay of the past will be re-enacted for a particular
purpose. Who benefits from this karmic repetition is determined by
the results of any new karma that is established between the people
concerned.

The HMVs can indicate a singular reoccurence of a karmic situation in which only one individual is involved, or it can signal an experience involving many situations and in which two or more people
participate.

Higher Master Vibrations are found *only* in the O Level Aspects
listed below. They are not located on P or C Levels.

1. Original Soul Print   OSP

2. Original Personality Vibration   OPV

3. Original Expressive Key   OEK

4. Vocational Motivator   VM
   (Derived by adding the unreduced Roots of the
   OSP+OPV+OEK+OP.)

5. Life Opportunities (Four parts)   L.Opp

6. Life Obstacles (Four parts)   L.Obs

7. Life Trinity Points (Three parts)   LT

The HMVs can be delineated and extracted by various computations. You must take care and time with them, as they can be easily
overlooked because of their varied and spread-out Chart locations.

CALCULATING THE HMVs

Now let's see how the HMVs are derived from the seven Aspects
above. You'll want to refer back to Peter Paul Connolly's complete
Basic Chart in Vol. I, Chapter 13, pp. 188–191.

Original Soul Print

The normal procedure for calculating the OSP is to add together
all the vowels in each name and reduce the total to a single digit:

$$1 \quad + \quad 4 \quad + \quad 3 \quad = 4 \text{ OSP}$$
$$10 \qquad 4 \qquad 12$$
$$5 \; 5 \qquad 1 \; 3 \qquad 6 \quad 6$$
PETER   PAUL   CONNOLLY

In looking for HMVs, we now add the *unreduced* numbers to obtain a two-digit total:

$$5+5+1+3+6+6 = \qquad\qquad 26 \text{ OSP (No HMV)}$$

Original Personality Vibration

$$7+2+9+7+3+3+5+5+3+3+7 = \qquad 54 \text{ OPV (No HMV)}$$

Original Expressive Key

$$7+5+2+5+9+7+1+3+3+3+6+5+5+6+3+3+7 = 80 \text{ OEK (No HMV)}$$

Vocational Motivator

$$8+18+17+20 = \qquad\qquad 63 \text{ VM (No HMV)}$$

Life Opportunities

L.Opp 1=9
L.Opp 2=3   L.Opp 1+L.Opp 2=   93 (No HMV)
L.Opp 3=3   L.Opp 2+L.Opp 3=   33 (No HMV)
L.Opp 4=1   L.Opp 3+L.Opp 4=   31 (No HMV)

Note: You do not work with the total of all four L.Opps here, but rather take them in pairs, so that you arrive at three unreduced totals. Notice that Peter has a 33 as a combination of L.Opps #2 and 3: this is *not* to be considered an EMV in this calculation.

Life Obstacles

L.Obs 1 = 7
L.Obs 2 = 1   L.Obs 1 + L.Obs 2 =   71 (No HMV)
L.Obs 3 = 6   L.Obs 2 + L.Obs 3 =   16 (No HMV)
L.Obs 4 = 6   L.Obs 3 + L.Obs 4 =   **66 (HMV)

Peter has an HMV here, comprised of L.Obs #3 and 4. His third Life Obstacle commences at age 43; this is also his Major Obstacle. His L.Obs #4 commences at age 52 and continues throughout his lifetime. Having an HMV at age 43 which will continue for the rest of his life is an excellent source of supportive energies which he will find very beneficial during this time period.

When an HMV is located in the Life Obstacles it indicates that during the specified time period you will receive support from another person or persons regarding your life goals. Peter's HMV shows that karma is *owed to him*. In a previous lifetime he was in some way prevented from reaching his karmic intention. Now in this lifetime he should be repaid with support, assistance, concern and generosity from those with whom he interacted before. The nature of this karmic cooperation is identified by the number of the HMV. As Peter's **66 is found in his Life Obstacles, it is intended to come in on a positive level.

Life Trinity Points

LT1 = 8
LT2 = 1   LT1 + LT2 =   81 (No HMV)
LT3 = 2   LT2 + LT3 =   12 (No HMV)

So we see that Peter has only ONE HMV in his Chart, located in the Life Obstacles.

INTERPRETING THE HMVs

Each of the HMVs reacts according to the Level of the person at the time a karmic situation is repeated. Each HMV is considered and delineated in the same way. For example, let's take Peter's **66:

1. The *first number*, which is identical to the second number, becomes the first consideration.

2. This first SIX indicates the last karmic experience that was focused on the SIX vibratory level.

3. The *second number*, identical to the first, indicates that the first karmic situation created in the previous life is destined to be balanced in this lifetime.

4. Each HMV is balanced by adding the two identical frequencies together and reducing the total to one digit, e.g.: **66 = 6 + 6 = 12 = 3.

5. THREE is the RECOGNITION NUMBER.

6. The first impact of any HMV is through its Recognition Number. This accounts for the subtle impact and input of the HMV.

7. When Peter's Karmic Replay begins, the HMV will first enter his life through the THREE vibration.

8. This THREE will enter with a FULL 100-DEGREE IMPACT and with no regard for Peter's level of sensitivity, whether it is positive or negative.

9. It can only enter when Peter becomes involved in the repeat karmic situation.

10. The HMV THREE brings all possibility of expression and will express itself according to the circumstances in which it becomes involved.

11. The force by which it can be monitored is generated by the equilibrium of the recipient at that time. It will change according to the balance level plus the situation, relationship, etc., he is experiencing at that time.

12. Each Recognition Number holds its influence for an identical number of 28-day segments. Peter's Recognition Number is

THREE, so he will feel its impact for: 3 × 28 = 84 days =
12 weeks = 3 months.

13. At the end of this time Peter will be involved in his Karmic
    Replay.

14. This Karmic Replay will be governed by the force of the *second* SIX. This SIX is computed like this: 6 × 28 = 168 days
    = 24 weeks = 6 months.

15. From the beginning to the end of this entire Karmic Period is
    a total of 252 days = 36 weeks = 9 months.

16. It is possible to have more than one HMV in your Chart.
    Each one should be calculated separately and analyzed in its
    own given time period.

17. When studying and interpreting HMVs it is essential that
    you consider the present activity of the Natal Chart Aspects
    and the Personal Life Cycles. Once this is done you will be
    able to understand how the HMVs are working and what
    they mean to you.

**FORTY-FOUR

1. Recognition Number = 4 + 4 = 8
2. 8 × 28 = 224 days = 32 weeks = 8 months
3. Karmic Replay is governed by the force of the 4
4. 4 × 28 = 112 days = 16 weeks = 4 months
5. Karmic Period = 12 months = 1 year

**FIFTY-FIVE

1. Recognition Number = 5 + 5 = 10 = 1
2. 1 × 28 = 28 days = 4 weeks = 1 month
3. Karmic Replay is governed by the force of the 5
4. 5 × 28 = 140 days = 20 weeks = 5 months
5. Karmic Period = 6 months

**SIXTY-SIX

1. Recognition Number = 6 + 6 = 12 = 3
2. 3 × 28 = 84 days = 12 weeks = 3 months
3. Karmic Replay is governed by the force of the 6
4. 6 × 28 = 168 days = 24 weeks = 6 months
5. Karmic Period = 9 months

**SEVENTY-SEVEN

1. Recognition Number = 7 + 7 = 14 = 5
2. 5 × 28 = 140 days = 20 weeks = 5 months
3. Karmic Replay is governed by the force of the 7
4. 7 × 28 = 196 days = 28 weeks = 7 months
5. Karmic Period = 12 months = 1 year

**EIGHTY-EIGHT

1. Recognition Number = 8 + 8 = 16 = 7
2. 7 × 28 = 196 days = 28 weeks = 7 months
3. Karmic Replay is governed by the force of the 8
4. 8 × 28 = 224 days = 32 weeks = 8 months
5. Karmic Period = 15 months = 1 year + 3 months

**NINETY-NINE

1. Recognition Number = 9 + 9 = 18 = 9
2. 9 × 28 = 252 days = 36 weeks = 9 months
3. Karmic Replay is governed by the force of the 9
4. 9 × 28 = 252 days = 36 weeks = 9 months
5. Karmic Period = 18 months = 1 year + 6 months

HMV INTERPRETATION CHART

HMV	RECOG. NO.	TIME	KARMIC REPLAY	TIME	KARMIC PERIOD
**44	8	8 mos.	4	4 mos.	1 year
**55	1	1 mo.	5	5 mos.	6 mos.
**66	3	3 mos.	6	6 mos.	9 mos.
**77	5	5 mos.	7	7 mos.	1 year
**88	7	7 mos.	8	8 mos.	1 year+3 mos.
**99	9	9 mos.	9	9 mos.	1 year+6 mos.

EFFECTS OF HMVs ON THE ASPECTS

As I mentioned before, HMVs are found *only* in these seven Aspects:

1. OSP
2. OPV
3. OEK
4. VM
5. L.Opp
6. L.Obs
7. LT

Now let's look at how the HMVs affect these Aspects and how to recognize them.

Original Soul Print

The OSP is the most sensitive location in which to find an HMV. It is a submerged Aspect, so unless the reduced digit of the OSP is an Extrovert number (see: Vol. I, Chapter 10, pp. 102–104), it can be difficult to express. Finding an HMV in this Aspect is an excellent sign! The additional HMV energies can help to reveal the intent and desire of the Original Soul Print.

Original Personality Vibration

At the time when the HMV is exact you will usually feel a total change in the behavior pattern. In preparation for the Karmic Replay the client will often express a completely different personality. When the HMV impacts on the OPV level it alerts past characteristics, which then appear to surface. This change is only as long as the length of the Karmic Period. In children, HMVs can be easily recognized. Partners in close relationships can detect subtle differences in attitude and behavior patterns. The HMV appears to support these changes. It's as though the client is forced to step back in time to regain his original footing. This change in outlook also affects his approach toward any given situation. It is only temporary and will subside quickly when the vibratory influence is released at the conclusion of the Karmic Period.

Original Expressive Key

In observing the impact of the HMV on this Aspect, you can expect many surprises! The basic rudiments of character and expression can become very difficult to understand. Appearances will deceive you: the client may appear to be conducting his life normally; then suddenly he may switch ideas and amaze everyone with radical new concepts. These could appear daring or even reckless. The impact of the HMV is causing the memory pattern to tap into previous behavior patterns in a past life. The client is still grounded in his normal behavior in the present, but his ideas and plans are now being influenced by his past-life OEK! This accounts for the unexpected behavior and attitudes when the HMV comes in on the OEK level.

Vocational Motivator

The HMV seldom seems hidden when it activates in the VM. There is a constant drive and urge to reach a satisfactory level of accomplishment. If the client finds it difficult to recognize and accept the steady flow of motivating vibrations in his life, he may experience doubt and frustration. Discontentment with opportunities offered, lack of concern about his present vocational status—these attitudes can lead you to think that the client has no ambition at all! It's far more beneficial for him if his vocational desire surfaces early in life, for once it is known the client can usually find success in his choice of work, career or profession.

Life Opportunities

The L.Opps, along with the L.Obs and Life Trinity Points, all fall within a specified time period. This provides a more accurate timing procedure for these three Aspects. After calculating when these Aspects occur, you can then be more precise in calculating the influence of the HMVs. In Peter's example you saw that his HMV was located in his L.Obs #3 and 4, from age 43 on. He can expect the first impact of his HMV the *first time* he experiences a Personal Life Cycle that is *identical* to his Recognition Number of THREE. The length of time each L.Opp, L.Obs or Life Trinity Point lasts determines whether or not the HMV will be repeated. If this occurs it offers further opportunity to achieve the karmic purpose of the HMV. The vibratory force of the L.Opp is given a tremendous jolt of energy by the HMV. It is definitely a positive factor, indicating that the Opportunity is meant to be utilized in this lifetime. I have discovered that an L.Opp HMV is usually the result of "carried-over" talents, which have been used to achieve a measure of success in a previous lifetime, but not necessarily the satisfaction to go along with it.

Life Obstacles

An HMV found in the Obstacles indicates that the client was prevented from fulfilling himself in a previous lifetime. If the blockage was created by others, then those who now present him with opportunity or remove barriers from his path may very well be the same souls who obstructed him before. If the blockage was self-created, the HMV will provide sufficient energy so that it will not occur again. It's always interesting to observe the cooperative and helpful people in your life, for they could very well be repaying karmic debts to you.

Life Trinity Points

Refer to Vol. I, Chapter 11, pp. 136–141, for a review of the LT points and how they affect you. The changing of the LT points and the influence of an HMV during these time periods can provide a dramatic turn of events. I have seen lives totally turned around by a Life Trinity Point HMV. The results of this combination of forces depends on what you are trying to do in life, whether it be with a relationship, career or whatever. The final result will be success. With an LT HMV operating, it's wise to recall the old saying: "Be careful what you wish for—you may get it!"

Personal Life Cycles

When the PLC is *identical to the Recognition Number,* the influence of these joint vibrations will create an impact for a period of time equal to the Recognition Number time (Recognition Number × 28 days). At the end of this period you will then go into the Karmic Replay, which is governed by the second number of the HMV. During the Karmic Replay you will repeat a similar patter of life experiences to those you lived out in a previous lifetime.

CHAPTER 14

UNDERSTANDING KARMA

Now that you have become familiar with the HMVs and their relationship to karma, I'd like to go into a bit more detail about this fascinating and vital subject that affects all of us.

There are of course two questions that everybody wants to know about karma?

1. Do I owe karma?
2. Is karma owed me?

The answer to both these questions is YES. I don't mean to be flippant, but karma is an elusive subject and everyone is involved in weaving his own destiny. Each thread is an experience in a different lifetime. The pattern of your life is the result of your skill as a karmic weaver to date.

At this point in the life of the human soul we have had many incarnations here on earth. You could say that we have all finished our Kindergarten many lifetimes ago and have passed through many grades of learning until we have finally graduated from the High School of existence. Earth is a University, and we are currently pursuing our various level of learning in it.

During the course of our many-lived education, we have all at one time or another incurred some type of karmic debt, just as everyone else has; therefore, inevitably, it's not a question of being in one category or the other—owing karma or being owed it. To one degree or another, we all owe and are owed karma.

The karmic obligations we carry are by no means equal. Some of us have produced better patterns than others; some of us have had difficulty in producing a good "weaving." The measure of karma differs for everyone. If you had no karmic obligations either way—you wouldn't be here now!

Life is a personal experience of the soul. The end result is to arrive at that level in which you realize that perfect contentment, understanding and love exist within you. This is the eventual reward that you give to yourself—to reach a point at which you are totally at peace with yourself and others—and with God.

When the soul at last stops searching for love in others and realizes that it *is* love, it becomes that love. It can no longer be broken into pieces or divided into relationships. It leaves behind all that was part of the Earth Educational System. Then it is one, it is all, it is everything. YOU ARE THIS LOVE NOW! Your Higher Self knows this truth. When your conscious mind comes to accept it, you will graduate with honors.

If you become too preoccupied with karma while studying your lessons here on earth, you may deprive yourself of all the opportunities life presents. If you decide to give nothing but the best, then only the best can happen to you! In giving yourself in love and service to others and not being overly concerned about what you receive in return, you are actually paying all your past karmic debts.

Some people worry that in order to pay off karmic obligations you have to pay them to the soul you owe them to in a past life. This can create a lot of anxiety! What have I done? Who did I do it to? What are my karmic debts? Are the people I owe in this lifetime with me? Who are they? How can I find them? All these questions become vitally important and the result is a headache! I have seen people refuse to accept the theory of reincarnation and karma altogether simply because they couldn't find answers to these questions.

Some people are privileged with certain degrees of extrasensory perception and can sometimes recognize someone from a past life when they meet them. But most of us don't have this gift and we feel frustrated when we try to work with karma.

Understanding how karma works will lead you to a way of accepting the theories of rebirth without feeling bewildered by it all.

THE LAW OF CAUSE AND EFFECT

To understand karma and how it works you must consider the Law of Cause and Effect. In simple terms: if karma is owed to me because of a cause, the balance of karmic law will eventually bring about the effect, which is the universal correcting procedure. Likewise, if I owe karma, I created the cause, and will then have to be a part of the correcting procedure by contributing to the effect.

Say for example that I live in Australia and my age is 42. By some act or deed in a previous lifetime I now owe you karma. But you happen to be born 41 years later! You are now one year old, a baby living near the beautiful vineyards of France. The question is: How do I pay you the karmic debt I owe you? Now let's complicate this a little further by saying you died yesterday.

The Law of Cause and Effect will still operate. We are all a part of this universal plan. Ultimately I *will* repay the karmic obligation. Not to you personally, but to someone who has need of my assistance. Haven't you ever been in the position where it seems that you're giving so much of yourself to so many people? What is important is the *actual balance* of the Universal Law. It's not just a matter of who repays whom or who did what to whom, although often when we are reborn we do encounter the same souls. When this happens we have the opportunity to personally pay our karmic debts, whether we understand them or not.

We should avoid personalizing karmic obligations; it doesn't always work that way. This explains why the human race can be so seemingly unfair and cruel. Although it might appear far more desirable to deliver your personal karmic obligations directly to their source, it can't always be that way. The Universal Law demands the balance, and as long as it is balanced by your act—then the karma is repaid. Human emotions have nothing at all to do with it. Man does not control the Universal Law of Balance. If he did, we would probably not be here at all.

So, once karma has established its cause, it will complete the effect. If the souls concerned are in this lifetime together, then the karmic drama will take place in that small group. But it is impossible for *all* the souls concerned to be together, so the Universal Law, like the rising sun, will continue its momentum and demand the balance from lifetime to lifetime.

The balance is all that matters. Whether you play a direct part in the balance is merely a choice which is not made here on earth. In giving, you receive. Knowing this should encourage you to give freely, for in doing so you will have all your past karmic debts paid in full.

SOUL MATES

Karma is personal. Souls are attracted to each other and will love each other throughout time. We all have soul mates, but unfortunately we do not always have the ideal circumstances for the perfect soul-mate relationship. The memory of the perfect relationship is registered in our past-life memory pattern. The soul deeply desires to make contact with its other half. Everyone yearns for their soul mate, but not everyone in every life experiences that wonderful contact. Still, the memory pattern urges with silent longing. We seek, pray, search and hope for that magnificent joining. If there is a constant yearning for union with the soul mate, this could be the result of a recent past-life experience in which two souls shared their lives.

Fortunately, we all survive the longing for the missing soul mate because we know that the severance is not forever. We live our lives, seeking our purpose, and fall in and out of love with other partners. The shedding of karma and all its obligations becomes important. It may be hard to realize that your soul mate could be the little baby in the high chair presently showing his future talent as a chef. You watch his artistry in throwing food together. He arouses your need to control and discipline, and as you lift him from his high chair you see that it's time to change his diaper. Now isn't it difficult to think that you and he might have walked the banks of the Nile in the moonlight long ago? That's what soul mates are all about!

The love that exists for all time has known all ways. We learn to love other souls for other reasons. We teach each other and learn from each other. During this process we make mistakes and the errors are known as karma. Forget your dread of karma and see it as the beautiful growth of human existence, the ultimate completion of which is love. To love and to give is to live and receive.

KARMA AND NUMBERS

Gnothology opens a door to understanding. Beyond this portal karma is portrayed through the complexity of numerical frequencies. Gnothology is the language of numbers. Through this fascinating language you are exposed to esoteric theories and philosophy. Belief in these theories is not necessary, much in the same way as you can speak a language but be unable to write it. But this numerical language can help you understand the workings of karma in your life and thus help you understand yourself and others better.

I suggest that you make karma a part of your thinking and living process. Your everyday actions can be a continual contribution to the Universal Law of karma. In this way you will receive an abundance of life opportunities. Karma can be fun: put out GOOD CAUSES and you will be the recipient of GOOD EFFECTS. You'll be a winner in life, for you could receive a beneficial effect that you haven't even expected. This may be thought of as luck, but don't you believe it!

CHAPTER 15

ANOTHER BEGINNING

Each new Chart is another beginning. Each beginning requires an end. But there is no end to the mystery of numbers, and so a Chart can never be complete. Each day it changes like the tide: vibrations come in and vibrations go out. The Gnothology Chart is the numerical portrait of a human being. He sits for his portrait and as he grows older, his Chart ages with him. It does not compliment nor reprimand him; it is a total picture of his karmic identity. It offers him the privilege of peering into invisible areas of life and of anticipating successes and failures.

You are the esoteric surgeon. As a Consultant you can dissect and explain the hidden mysteries locked within the Chart. With skill and sensitivity you can probe into dark, undiscovered areas and expose the brilliance of the workings of karma. You can also use your esoteric talents to immunize the young and protect them from future hazards.

Modern medicine has taught us that early immunization can prevent certain diseases at a later age. Children can benefit not only from medical immunization but from the esoteric "vaccination" of knowledge based on their numerical Charts. My third volume of Gnothology will be entirely devoted to the sensitivity and interpretation of children's Charts. The process of delineation will be identical, regardless of age. Consequently, the procedures of Chart composition can be found in Vols. I and II of *The Connolly Book of Numbers*. This book will help teacher, parent and counselor to understand the many changes that take place in the child through the vital learning years toward early maturity. This book will also be a handbook for the young adult who would like insight into his own life path.

Always remember that Gnothology is an esoteric language. Your command of this language depends on the diligence of your initial study and on the skillful and sensitive application of this study. It has been my purpose to teach you to become proficient in the language of numbers. I hope that you will become an excellent teacher and counselor. Use your knowledge with sensitivity and you will always be in demand. Until we meet again I wish you success and long happy hours of study.

THE GNOTHOLOGIST

He knows the language of numbers and man,
Creating his Charts with professional skill;
Trying to open the secret of life,
Looking for karma yet to fulfill.

He sees the purpose and journey of soul;
Wrapped in the babe the secret lies.
Summers counted and winters lost
Will never equal the tears he cries.

He looks for Cycles to change the way,
How they work and lose their power;
Opportunity comes and goes,
Lost before the midnight hour.

Obstacles loom and dull the day;
The Chart is searched for truth and love.
Vibrational forces alter the path,
Panic comes with push and shove.

Fortunate days forget to transpire,
Why don't they know they are sorely missed?
The magic of knowing is making it work,
More knowledge is needed, so he must persist.

Karma is woven in memory and life,
A pattern that's colored and shows the pain.
How does the Gnothologist know so much
From a birthday and my lover's name?

—Eileen Connolly

INFLUENTIAL NUMBERS IN YOUR LIFE

In our busy everyday lives, we are aware of all the numbers that seem to infest our days like buzzing insects, but we tend to forget that *all* numbers have power and energy. Those closest and most important to us, those we use or find ourselves under the influence of every day, have vibratory influences that we should be aware of.

So here are the numerical secrets of some of those everyday numbers you take for granted. They shouldn't be overlooked or ignored!

YOUR TELEPHONE

Your telephone number is important: it has its own vibratory influence on your day-to-day life. For example, if your telephone number adds up to SEVEN, you'll attract a different kind of caller than you will if it adds up to FIVE.

A home and business phone will have entirely different influences. Consider them as separate calculations and remember that each phone has its own "personality" and "appetite" for certain types of conditions and callers.

To calculate your phone Number, add the individual digits together and reduce. Do *not* include the area code, for you share this number with many thousands of others. Also, do not reduce Master Numbers *11, *22 or *33. For example:

$$(213)\ 467\text{-}3296 = 4+6+7+3+2+9+6 = 37 = 10 = 1$$

If this were your telephone number, your Number would be ONE. Now here's a list of conditions and telephone behavior you can expect from your telephone.

ONE

A ONE phone will attract callers who need to speak directly to you. Your phone bill can be quite expensive, for people will want to discuss things in detail.

Home Phone ONE

Not so good, unless you live alone. Other family members will feel that you monopolize the phone.

Business Phone ONE

If you prefer your secretary or other employees to answer your phone, you could experience difficulty with callers who insist on speaking to you personally.

Care and Feeding of Telephone ONE

Requires personal attention for long periods of time. Repeats your name over and over until you're sick of it.

TWO

This telephone attracts those who like in-depth conversations. Many secrets are revealed on a TWO phone. Other callers are used to hearing the busy tone.

Home Phone TWO

I would suggest a change of number or an extra telephone! Otherwise you may lose some of your calls from long periods of being busy.

Business Phone TWO

Depending on the nature of the business, I wouldn't recommend a TWO phone, as it has a tendency to attract problems.

Care and Feeding of Telephone TWO

Thrives on dilemmas! Gets hungry for who did what to whom. Difficult to get away from, especially when you have other things to do.

THREE

Good for intellectual and social communication. Have your pen and notepad handy. Invitations, telephone orders, club meetings, important dates all come through the THREE phone.

Home Phone THREE

Bright and cheery. Friends call with invitations or new ideas. An element of surprise when the phone rings! Appointments, professional meetings, interviews, etc.

Business Phone THREE

Good business communication. The caller receives a precise but pleasant vibration. A THREE phone can be a good asset to any business or profession.

Care and Feeding of Telephone THREE

Gets up early, goes to bed late! Busy attracting last-minute details. Likes surprises and good news. Loves precision and detail.

FOUR

The FOUR phone is like an anchor. It can't deal with short, curt messages. You'll find that if you have an answering machine your callers will leave long, detailed messages.

HOME PHONE FOUR

Using the phone will save you a lot of driving! You can accomplish lots of work just by using the phone. Good for getting to the bottom of things.

BUSINESS PHONE FOUR

Not many mistakes should slip by here! You will gather plenty of information and will be respected by your callers. Gives an air of reliability.

CARE AND FEEDING OF TELEPHONE FOUR

Good digestion! Can absorb almost anything. Will demand every detail and then check it again. Loves plain facts for dessert.

FIVE

You'll never know what or whom to expect on the FIVE phone! An answering machine might help sort out the many calls you will receive. It's interesting and colorful and always ringing!

HOME PHONE FIVE

The ideal number to have if you like to talk to different people. It will constantly attract all kinds of calls for many different reasons. Can be both entertaining and tiring!

Business Phone FIVE

Your phone will always be ringing! A good business phone, but be sure you have a competent operator, otherwise confusion could set in. Attracts long-distance calls.

Care and Feeding of Telephone FIVE

Loves calls from every direction. Thrives on constant ringing. Emotional levels, tears and laughter are delicious. Dislikes serious levels.

SIX

The SIX phone attracts serious information. Conversations are quite meaningful. The owner of the SIX phone will always feel the need to think about the call afterward.

Home Phone SIX

Can be more entertaining than a soap opera! Deep breaths are needed after calls are through. It is a demanding number: you may feel exhausted after use.

Business Phone SIX

Patience is required on a SIX phone. You must be able to listen and empathize. Like a roller coaster, there'll be many ups and downs. Needs good management.

Care and Feeding of Telephone SIX

Lots of spicy snacks! Constant feeding but no fancy stuff! Can change diet often with no ill effects. Adaptable as long as it is plain cooking.

SEVEN

A sensitive vibration conducive to philosophical chit-chat. Nothing seems to be achieved. Things are left up in the air with no decisions. Difficult to get a commitment on SEVEN.

HOME PHONE SEVEN

Answering the SEVEN phone is a commitment in itself! You may feel that you are getting tied up or involved when you really don't want to. Makes you think!

BUSINESS PHONE SEVEN

Good for lengthy discussions. Not good for commitments. People are difficult to pin down. Can be frustrating. Not good for quick, fast decisions.

CARE AND FEEDING OF TELEPHONE SEVEN

Finicky is the word for phone SEVEN! Never quite sure what it wants. If left alone it won't eat at all. Needs to be spoon-fed; sometimes spits it back.

EIGHT

A demanding vibration that requires the facts. Can bring in exciting information. Does not have a sympathetic level, therefore it may seem heartless at times.

HOME PHONE EIGHT

If you are doing business at home you have a good number. If not, you will attract people who seem to be in a hurry and also sales calls out of nowhere.

Business Phone EIGHT

Excellent for business communication. Wise to have full details ready by the phone. Will attract money, orders and appointments.

Care and Feeding of Telephone EIGHT

Enormous appetite for money in any denomination. Likes checks for dessert! Loves to hear business talk while eating. Drinks plenty of success.

NINE

The keen vibrations of the NINE phone like to extend themselves as far as possible. Will bring in news from distant places likes to respond by calling back.

Home Phone NINE

Watch your phone bill! Long-distance calls are forever piling up! A need to make long-distance contacts. You will also attract calls from far away.

Business Phone NINE

Excellent for business. Be careful not to talk needlessly or you'll have to pay the cost. Good for initiating new contacts and attracting new business.

Care and Feeding of Telephone NINE

Could have a continental appetite! Likes long-distance drinks. Loves the various accents of people from far places. Always on the run.

*ELEVEN

A perfect vibration for the silent, serious telephone lover. This phone will attract meaningful conversations. I think it dislikes *being* a telephone! It's reluctant to be cheery.

HOME PHONE *ELEVEN

Good for outbursts of genius or emotion. Dramatic influences, a confessional. Your words will be remembered, so think before you speak.

BUSINESS PHONE *ELEVEN

You may find that customers derive a great deal of satisfaction in confiding in you. You'll feel compelled to relate exactly how your products work, down to the last detail.

CARE OF FEEDING OF TELEPHONE *ELEVEN

Wants full details of ingredients and how you prepared and cooked the meal. Fussy and unappreciative. Everything must be served correctly.

*TWENTY-TWO

Attracts success and hard work. An exacting vibration with little tolerance for mistakes. Always have your facts straight, for it won't put up with weakness or excuses.

HOME PHONE *TWENTY-TWO

A demanding vibratory influence. You will want the facts. They will want the facts! Many opportunities will be presented on a *22 phone. Be ready to act.

BUSINESS PHONE *TWENTY-TWO

Just what you need for a fast-moving business. Attracts money, orders and people. An expansive vibration that is geared toward success.

CARE AND FEEDING OF TELEPHONE *TWENTY-TWO

Robust appetite. Likes to feast. Wants variety and with the right silverware can create repeated success.

*THIRTY-THREE

A highly sensitive vibration which will bring in calls that require much thought. No casual calls on a *33 phone! Its strong energy level will attract unusual and unexpected contacts.

HOME PHONE *THIRTY-THREE

You will have many memories of telephone conversations with a *33 phone. Unusual situations and circumstances will occur. Powerful for decision-making. Karma can easily get on the line!

BUSINESS PHONE *THIRTY-THREE

Like a magnet your number will attract unusual business opportunities. Must be ready to act quickly. No procrastination on phone *33!

CARE AND FEEDING OF TELEPHONE *THIRTY-THREE

Can change from day to day. Has unusual tastes but will show gratitude. Will ask for strange things to be served. Have them cooking on the stove.

YOUR HOME ADDRESS

This is the influence you immediately feel when you walk into your home. You felt it when you first looked at the house. Those who visit feel it every time they come to see you. The vibrations are governed by the *number* of the house. This number remains with the house and in turn affects those living in it.

Each home attracts certain types of people. It's good to consider this when contemplating a move. Next time you're house-hunting keep this in mind and see how you feel as you walk inside each place you examine. Maybe you are ready to make a change! Not just to a new house, but to a new way of living.

To calculate your Home Number, add the individual digits of your address together and reduce. For example:

11209 La Maida Street $= 1+1+2+0+9 = 13 = 4$

If this were your address, your Home Number would be FOUR.

ONE

A sense of independence. The residents have the opportunity to be a vital part of the community. They usually take pride in the appearance of the home. Attracts strong, independent people. Not too neighborly until they get to know you.

TWO

Warm and friendly. Family-oriented. Occupants like to garden and have an occasional chat and enjoy social and club activities. Good home for settling down. Usually has a long occupancy. Attracts families with children, cats and dogs. They like to have friends visit and will always offer a helping hand.

THREE

Up-to-the-minute furnishings. Bright and well decorated. An encouraging artistic influence. Telephone likes to ring with interesting callers. Attracts artistic and professional people. Always busy, newspapers in the yard. Cheerful occupants, involved in many things.

FOUR

A solid-looking house. You get the feeling of "home." Looks like it would be safe and comfortable. Visitors stay a little longer than expected. A feeling of instant welcome. Attracts homemakers, people who like to cook and who offer you second helpings. Comfy beds and lots of trees and plants.

FIVE

A feeling of space and light. Sparkling windows, drapes open wide. Minimum outside work. Perhaps a drawing board in the dining room, expensive cushions and wooden boxes. Attracts busy, creative people. Lots of comings and goings. Conditions are always changing. Sophistication surrounds this house. Straighten your tie as you ring the doorbell.

SIX

A well-established home, respected in the neighborhood. Occupied by reliable folks with family traditions who know the area well. They'll volunteer to pick up your prescription. Outside in the garden on weekends. Attracts married couples. Path swept every morning. Law and order prevails here. Extremely polite; clean, shiny car outside or neatly parked in the garage.

SEVEN

Peaceful home, tranquil and tastefully furnished. An air of dignity, with good books lying around. Easy and relaxed, educated conversations. You never see a soap opera on the television screen! Attracts intellectual people. An air of serenity pervades this home, with quiet music. Always a genuine smile from its occupants.

EIGHT

An important home, well maintained and furnished. Each room has its own identity and character. Attractively painted, with an excellent doorbell and porch lamp. Impressive as you walk in. Attracts established people. Everything in order. Refreshments served on good china. An experienced couple who know what they're doing and how they got here.

NINE

A nice home anyone would love. Neutral tones and pleasant surroundings. Fresh flowers and a perfect guest room. Always a welcome from this home. Birthday cards all written and ready to go! Attracts disciplined people with a low profile. Genuine affection here —a happy home. These people truly enjoy visiting.

*ELEVEN

Smoke comes out of the chimney on chilly evenings. Floppy cushions and dog hairs. Sparkling ceramics and homemade muffins. Easy and relaxed. Clean towels in the bathroom; just move the dog out and it'll be OK. Attracts kind, genuine people, who are willing to move over on the couch. They can always put you up for the night. A good shoulder to cry on. They may be preoccupied, so help yourself! Good, loving folks.

*TWENTY-TWO

This has got to be the best-looking house in the area. Fancy gate, impressive door, large hallway. Someone shouts "come in" and you could find yourself in the closet! Obviously everything is expensive. Attracts everyone! Seriously, this is the house of the powerful *22. Lots of thought and effort has gone into this beauty. It is beautifully decorated and furnished. The owners are very proud of their achievements.

*THIRTY-THREE

A quiet home. Blinds are down halfway. Pencils and paper fill the dining-room table. Cold coffee mugs, half-filled. Good leather briefcase with a cat lying inside asleep. Tinkling chimes outside, soft music in and CBS News blasting away. Attracts quiet people. They're content to work, read poetry and fall asleep listening to Bach. Plenty of health food available and always a bottle of wine.

You must have a sense of humor when selecting a home. The house provides the vibratory influence of its address; *you* create the atmosphere. Your home is a coloring book, waiting for you to color it your way.

Apartments, Hotels and Condominiums

I've seen students become confused when attempting to delineate apartment numbers or hotel room numbers. Actually, it's very simple: you use the number on the *door*—not the collective number that some housing complexes have.

Apartment numbers or room numbers identified by a letter before or after them are simply calculated using the numerical equivalent of the letter. For instance:

Apartment 3-F $= 3 + 6 = 9$

Apartment C28 $= 3 + 2 + 8 = 13 = 4$

If your apartment number includes a ½ or a ¼, it's a little more complicated. Let's say your address is 14½ Maple St. Your Home Number is FIVE (1 + 4). The fraction is then divided as follows:

1. The ONE on top always belongs to the *neighbor* who has the full number (14).

2. The bottom number (TWO) is *yours*.

3. You are living in a FIVE home (apartment), which will have the true FIVE vibration.

4. The TWO indicates how you should relate to your neighbor.

5. If your number were 14¼, the same principle would apply— the FOUR would be yours and would guide you in your relationship with your neighbor.

YOUR STATE

To arrive at workable numbers for the STATE you live in, you must discover the vibrations of the first three Aspects of the state (yes, states can have Charts just like people!). The State of CALIFORNIA, for example, has the following:

```
 1  +  9  +  6  +    9 + 1   = 26 = 8 OSP (2 & 6 Rooting)
 C     A     L  I  F  O  R  N  I  A
 3  +  3  +  6  +  9 + 5      = 26 = 8 OPV (2 & 6 Rooting)
 3 + 1 + 3 + 9 + 6 + 6 + 9 + 5 + 9 + 1  = 52 = 7 OEK (5 & 2 Rooting)
```

In analyzing this calculation, first notice that the OSP and OPV have identical Rootings, the result being an EIGHT on both levels. What kind of an EIGHT? You can discover this by looking at the TWO and SIX Rooting, which determines the nature of the EIGHT.

The TWO and SIX Rooting tells you that the State of California was meant to prosper and will always attract business and industry. Gold mines were part of its beginning, and today banks and large corporations grow bigger every day. Not for nothing is California called "The Golden State." The Rootings of its OSP indicate that with cooperation and harmony this Aspect will activate and reach its Original Purpose, which is found in the consolidated EIGHT.

California's OSP is not hindered by an Introverted OPV. Instead you have the identical vibration with identical Rooting, which supports the needs of the OSP. The OSP can manifest itself easily, for it duplicates its intent on the Extroverted OPV level. Again, with cooperation and harmony (now they must be evident on the outside), the OPV will activate and provide the circumstances desired by the OSP.

Does California offer cooperation in business and finance? Of course—that's one reason why millions of people from all over the world have come to this state to become involved in commerce.

With the third level of the OEK, the question is: "How does California express all that we have learned about it from the two previous levels?" With the SEVEN. The OEK of SEVEN indicates that the influence California extends is in fact quite subtle. It suggests that many sensitive people have settled here because of this influence. You can also see that on a large scale California thinks deeply and attracts people with this kind of personality. This sensitivity can be seen in the early industry of movie-making and other creative arts. California's spirituality is wide and deep, allowing free choice to the beliefs of all. This spirituality can be observed in the art of the state and the way it has welcomed and sheltered millions of people and their varied spectrum of religious beliefs.

The OEK's SEVEN Rooting of FIVE and TWO explains how all these things came about. The FIVE is the actual vibration that initiates the attraction—it welcomes all people, all situations, all types of art and personal expression. The TWO amplifies the energies of the two TWOs in the OSP and OPV levels, creating a feeling of personal cooperation which helps newcomers to establish themselves and become part of the sensitive OEK of SEVEN.

It's a good idea to analyze the states you are associated with: the one you were born in, if different from where you're living now; and states in which you do business or have relatives or friends living. Everyone is affected by the general influence of the state they live in. You can extend your study beyond the OSP, OPV and OEK to the Original Plan, if you wish. To find this number, you'll have to do a little research and discover the month, day and year your state was first admitted into the Union. If you read about the history of the state, you'll be able to see how these numerical Aspects have guided its destiny since that time.

YOUR COUNTRY

The Original Plan for the United States can be delineated by taking the month, day and year of the signing of the Declaration of Independence, July 4, 1776:

JULY = 7

   4 = 4

1776 = 1776

         1787 = 23 = 5 OP

The Original Plan of our country, then, is the FIVE, the vibration of personal freedom and expression!

USING THE INFLUENTIAL NUMBERS IN YOUR LIFE

All states and countries have an Original Plan, as well as the other three Aspects you've just worked with for California. I mentioned earlier that you were not influenced by the Area Code number of your telephone because many people share that number. However, you *are* influenced by the numbers of your state and country. The reason for this is that the NAMES of the state and country have an overall influence on all those residing within their borders.

If you've lived in another state or country, you can tune in to the vibratory differences immediately when you arrive there. The same applies to the cities or towns in which you live. All these vibratory forces affect your personal levels. Some people feel these influences to such an extent that after trying to live in another town or state or country, they will eventually move back. There have even been cases in which gravely ill persons recovered their health after being returned to their home state and city.

You can make use of the numbers in your environment to guide and stimulate you. Your Telephone Number, Address or Apartment Number, City and State Number, are all exerting vibrational influences in your life which you can take advantage of.

For example, before you make a major decision to move to another city or state, ask yourself, "What do I want from the area I intend to move to?"

1. If you want to satisfy your OSP and find inner happiness, choose a place whose OEK is complementary to yours.

2. If you're looking for a new job or planning to open a business, then find the OSP of the place and compare it with your OEK.

3. If you wish to gain experience, find a place whose OP is identical to yours.

By following these guidelines you'll discover whether or not you're going to the right place to satisfy your present needs. When making these kinds of decisions keep in mind that your current Personal Life Cycle will determine whether or not you are *ready* to make the move!

EILEEN CONNOLLY'S
MYSTICAL FOCHAADAMS

The MYSTICAL FOCHAADAMS are a new and exciting form of divination which can reveal esoteric wisdom and guidance through the interpretations of the symbols portrayed. Eileen Connolly, author, lecturer and teacher, has spent years researching and developing this unique system. In 1974 she named them with a mystical word derived from two languages, Hebrew and Tibetan:

FO	Fohat	Essence of cosmic electricity
CHAA	Chabad	Wisdom, reason and intuition
DAMS	Yidams	Phenomenal projections of a person's inherent energy

Like many other forms of divination—Tarot, Numerology, Astrology, etc.—the Mystical Fochaadams are not to be considered as a means of mere fortune-telling, but rather as a modern tool to help you discover, analyze and make meaningful decisions based on your higher level of consciousness. Throwing the Mystical Fochaadams and being prepared to recognize future trends as the results of present activities will lead you into areas of interpretation that will greatly enhance your esoteric skill, sensitivity and intuition.

Ancient symbols were designed to lead the higher consciousness into esoteric areas without the restrictions of form and reason. They were intended to trigger the student's higher vibrations, thus opening his awareness to areas of philosophy hitherto unknown to him. Various images and shapes formed the languages of the ancients. The discovery of how certain symbols, like words, have been used by many different cultures was the key to mastering the whole system.

Words can often obliterate the vast knowledge contained in symbology. Working with symbols eliminates the need for words as such, allowing emotion in its purest form to reach and stimulate the higher senses directly.

The Mystical Fochaadams allow access into the world of esoteric wisdom and can give you the ability to understand and make use of this wisdom, based on your own personal level of sensitivity. Master the Mystical Fochaadams and you will always have a friend. Like the Tarot, they can be used both for yourself or with clients.

Your Mystical Fochaadams consist of a beautiful esoteric throw cloth and a collection of unique updated symbols on a group of throwing pieces. They are simple to use and can reveal the past, present and future with amazing accuracy.

The Mystical Fochaadams enhance and complement other divination systems: they can confirm and clarify many areas of interest opened by the Tarot, answering questions regarding relationships, business, financial matters, etc. You will find them an invaluable addition to your esoteric tools and discover an oracle of hitherto unsuspected dimensions.

Dr. Connolly also conducts International Certification Courses in the following subjects: Gnothology, Tarot and the Mystical Fochaadams.

* Lectures	* Seminars
* Workshops	* Intensive Study

For information on wholesale and retail sales and courses, write to:

Stone Circle Productions
Richmond Road
Rt. 2, Box 76
Linexa, VA 23089

Eileen Connolly's Mystical Fochaadams

THE NEWEST FORM OF DIVINATION

•Simple to use

•Amazing accuracy

•Reveals past, present
and future

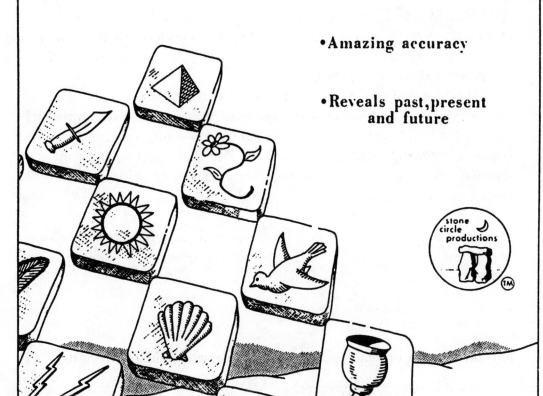

stone
circle
productions